LIGHT
WARRIOR

LIGHT
WARRIOR

Connecting with the
Spiritual Power of
Fierce Love

KYLE GRAY

HAY HOUSE

Carlsbad, California • New York City • London
Sydney • Johannesburg • Vancouver • New Delhi

Published and distributed in the United States by: Hay House, Inc.: www.hayhouse .com® • Published and distributed in Australia by: Hay House Australia Pty. Ltd.: www.hayhouse.com.au • Published and distributed in the United Kingdom by: Hay House UK, Ltd.: www.hayhouse.co.uk • Published and distributed in the Republic of South Africa by: Hay House SA (Pty), Ltd.: www.hayhouse.co.za • Distributed in Canada by: Raincoast Books: www.raincoast.com • Published in India by: Hay House Publishers India: www.hayhouse.co.in

Cover and interior design: Leanne Siu Anastasi

The author of this book does not dispense medical advice or prescribe the use of any technique as a form of treatment for physical, emotional, or medical problems without the advice of a physician, either directly or indirectly. The intent of the author is only to offer information of a general nature to help you in your quest for emotional, physical, and spiritual well-being. In the event you use any of the information in this book for yourself, the author and the publisher assume no responsibility for your actions.

Library of Congress Control Number: 2017948499

Tradepaper ISBN: 978-1-4019-5347-8

10 9 8 7 6 5 4 3 2 1
1st edition, October 2017

Printed in the United States of America

*For Louise Hay, without whom this
work would not be possible.*

*I am eternally grateful. Thank you
for being a light to us all.*

Guardians of the four corners,

Mother in the Earth, Father in the Sky,

Angels, archangels, ancestors of time and ancestors of place,

Thank you for your blessings and your direction.

Thank you for guiding the warriors back to their light.

May this work be a catalyst for great healing and change.

May all of those ready to light up be guided to heal their darkness.

Aho!

CONTENTS

PREFACE

For thousands of years a halo of light has been used to show holy figures in the religions and spiritual traditions of the world. In the Bible, angels are described as beings of burning light. In the traditional paintings of Japanese Shintoism, saints are depicted emerging from caves with light bursting behind them. Aboriginal cave paintings show ancestor spirits' heads surrounded by a wheel of light. Light has actually been seen around saints and spiritual teachers, and many people who have had spiritual experiences have also reported seeing light, whether at the end of a tunnel in a near-death experience or surrounding an angel who has visited them in a vision or dream.

Light gives the impression of godliness, peace and love. It is viewed as a sign of power, strength and spiritual achievement. And it is now commonly accepted in modern spirituality that light is also within us – every one of us.

Go to any yoga class and you'll hear the Sanskrit salutation *Namaste* being shared by student and teacher alike. It means 'the light in me bows to the light in you'. And in the psychic field, the phrase 'love and light' has become a common way to sign off at the end of a message, article or gathering.

We are becoming more aware that light is all around us, light is within us, light is who we are.

So why is our world often so dark? Why should this be, when I believe – I *know* – that the universe is love?

This love stuff is the real story, but many down here on this planet have forgotten. And because they've forgotten, they've begun to live their earthly journeys in a mysteriously challenging way that has created a lot of suffering for other people, for animals and for the Earth.

I believe the universe is trying to rectify this – trying to heal the Earth. So now more than ever it needs light. It is calling out for it. I believe we're all hearing that call, for we're all expressions of the universe who are having an earthly experience right now.

The call could come as a feeling, or an intense emotion, or a prompt to do something. It could be a desire to become a more positive person, to change our body or our habits, to heal an addiction. It could be a desire to help others.

For years, souls who have heard this call have been named 'lightworkers', a term representative of the incredible light they have within them and the work they feel they're here to do.

It's now time for us all to answer the call – to shine, to dispel the darkness and let love lead. The fact that you have this book in your hands right this moment means you're already shining and you're ready to shine some more. Right now, this second, I want to honour you. I humbly bow to you. The light in me bows to the light in you.

So, how do we do it? How do we respond to the call?

All healing begins within. You've probably heard that before, right? And it's true. So, in order to heal the outer world, we begin on the inside – with ourselves. All that we do for ourselves is actually for the world. So we respond to the call for light by facing our own fear. We respond by lighting up our own shadow. When we face our own darkness, we remove darkness from the world. It's as simple as that – although it's not always that simple.

What you are holding in your hands is a guide to becoming a light in the world. A pathway that I like to call *warriorship*.

ACKNOWLEDGEMENTS

I am so grateful to be sharing my life and work with the world. It's taken a whole team of us to enable this book to become what it is today.

Huge thanks to Michelle Pilley, my commissioning editor and spiritual guide. Without your incredible insights and direction, this book wouldn't be half as good!

Thank you to the edit angel, Lizzie Henry, for taking my words and making them magical. You are so gifted.

Thanks to Drew Barnes for the fantastic cover photo and for patiently guiding me to reveal myself and nothing else.

Thank you to Leanne Siu Anastasi for working hard on the book design and Julie Oughton for direction on everything editorial. It's been a joy.

I also want to thank everyone else at Hay House UK who has supported my growth and also the Wrage family in Germany, who have helped me create a voice in Europe.

To my mum, Diane, who has been a never-ending support on this journey and for putting up with my roars, mood swings and everything else that comes with raising a warrior spirit – I love you.

Chapter 1
NOT ALL ANGELS ARE FLUFFY

'The essence of warriorship, or the essence of human bravery, is refusing to give up on anyone or anything.'
CHÖGYAM TRUNGPA

The word 'warrior' had never really been part of my vocabulary until I took up yoga. In yoga, 'warrior poses' are frequent – in fact I don't think I've ever been to a dynamic yoga class that didn't have one. So for the last eight years I've been doing these poses quite a lot, yet until recently I'd never considered myself a warrior. When I thought about warriors, I thought about armour and battles. Not very spiritual. Or so I thought.

For me, as for many people, being spiritual and being a warrior were concepts that couldn't have been further apart. There's a widespread idea that being spiritual is all about love, light and fairy dust, whatever the circumstances. I have to be honest, though – I've not always resonated with pastels or all-white clothing, or unicorns (as cool as the idea may be), *or* being able to ignore someone when they're being rude (I've always struggled with that one).

1

Even worse, while touring my last book, *Raise Your Vibration*, I realized that being a lightworker had become a new trend. I knew that many of the people who resonated with that term were doing incredible work sharing their light with the world, but I also recognized that others were just jumping on the label as if it was a new fashion and taking action to change the world was as easy as dying your hair pink.

For me, being a lightworker isn't about posing, it's about *doing the work.* If we sign up for the mission to support the growth of our planet, we have to turn up for it. This turning up isn't about posting our latest crystal purchase on Instagram (although I've been known to do this), it's about showing up for our spiritual practice, facing our shit not putting glitter on it, and aligning ourselves with the universe. It's about service. It's about being the embodiment of an angel on Earth.

When I was considering this idea, it got me thinking. Not all angels are fluffy. Not all angels sit on a cloud playing the harp. Some angels wear armour and carry weapons. They are fierce warriors. Look at the best-known angel there is, Archangel Michael. If you google image him, you'll see a strong and ferociously handsome angel dressed in armour, holding a sword, usually with some fire on it, standing on top of Lucifer.

The story goes (in my own words but based on the Book of Revelation) that Lucifer (who became 'the devil') was causing a bit of a riot up in heaven. He thought he was sharper and cooler than God. God supposedly wasn't happy about this and so he called upon Michael and his legion of angels to take care of the pest.

This is a powerful allegory showing that *love* (in this case Michael) is much more powerful than fear (in this case the devil). It's a tale that shows us that warriors can be fiercely powerful and yet completely fuelled by love.

Angels are warriors of love. They have to be warriors to help us overcome our own dilemmas, traumas and fears. So, if lightworkers are embodiments of angels on Earth, they don't always have to be the fluffy type of angel – they can be the fierce kind too. They can be light warriors.

This idea helped me because I'd often wondered if I was 'good enough' to be spiritual. Let's face it, though I really believe in helping others and living a life with integrity and purpose, I've not always been passive in my approach. To be honest, I've been a bit of a badass.

I checked the dictionary definition of 'warrior' and I found: '(especially in former times) a brave or experienced soldier or fighter'. The synonyms were just as intense: 'fighter, soldier, fighting man, serviceman, combatant, brave'.

But the warriorship I was thinking about wasn't about fighting with your fists or fighting with your mind, it was about connecting with the incredible power of spirit within to overcome darkness, challenge and fear. So I looked up 'spiritual warrior':

> *The term 'spiritual warrior' is used in*
> *Tibetan Buddhism for one who combats the*
> *universal enemy: self-ignorance (avidya),*
> *the ultimate source of suffering according*
> *to Buddhist philosophy. A heroic being*
> *with a brave mind and ethical impulse.*

Bam. There it was.

Light Warriors in Action

A lightworker is a soul who hears the cry to help change the world and a light warrior is a soul who consciously chooses to respond.

We live in a world where light warriors have made great healing shifts and are still doing so today. They don't have to come from a particular tradition or religion. There are many of them all over the planet, and some of them don't even know that they're warriors – they're just responding to the call to change the world. Most of us don't know about these unsung heroes either, but there are many light warriors we do know and whose work we can use as inspiration for our own spiritual journey.

I'm thinking of people like Gandhi, who, though he fought for Indian independence from the British Empire, was totally dedicated to non-violence. He stood so strong and encouraged so many to stand with him, and even though he went to hell and back, his work did help his cause, and he didn't lift a finger, he lifted his heart. That's what being a light warrior is all about.

Another example is Martin Luther King Jr, the American Baptist minister who had complete faith in God as he encouraged non-violent action to change America through the civil rights movement. It gives me goosebumps to think of the work he did at a time when people were being falsely accused, imprisoned, beaten and even murdered just because of the colour of their skin. He *knew* that he could make a difference and he devoted his life to helping make his vision a reality. I bow to the spirit of Martin Luther King! Thank you!

I also think of other spiritual warriors, some more extreme than others, like the Vietnamese monk Thích Quảng Đức, who set himself on fire in protest against the persecution of Buddhist monks in 1963. A photograph of this was published in newspapers around the world, resulting in international pressure on the Vietnamese regime to change their treatment of Buddhists.

I once saw an interview on *The Oprah Winfrey Show* with Thích Nhất Hạnh, another Vietnamese spiritual warrior and a personal hero of mine, who led a peaceful protest against the Vietnamese civil war. In the interview he discussed his relationship with Martin Luther King and revealed that he'd written him a letter explaining that Thích Quảng Đức's self-immolation was not suicide. He said that it was 'through compassion' that he'd taken what appeared to be such a drastic step: 'It was an act of love and not despair.'

I don't feel self-immolation is what we need to do to make a difference, even though I can see that what Thích Quảng Đức did was an act of true courage. We don't have to act on a global scale either. Being a light warrior can simply be vowing to change your part of the world and being an active light wherever you are – a light that can inspire others.

Recently, many first peoples of the United States came together in the Standing Rock Native American Reservation in North and South Dakota, standing together with the Great Spirit to protect their sacred land and water from an oil pipeline that was likely to pollute the water and threaten nature. Though they weren't as successful as they'd hoped, they have inspired people around the world.

Another inspirational light warrior is one of my personal heroines, Louise Hay. After being diagnosed with cancer in her late fifties, she felt the call to do mental, emotional and spiritual work instead of going down the medical route. She felt that her cervical cancer was the product of deep resentment that was connected to emotional and sexual abuse from her childhood. She took to making daily affirmations, releasing anger, forgiving others and doing daily 'mirror work', where she told herself regularly (as she still does) that she loved and approved of herself. And after several months of this, she was able to get the medical professionals to agree with what she already knew – that she was free of cancer.

Louise was already a healer, but this gave her work a new understanding and authenticity that allowed her to help people find the emotional causes behind physical ailments and the new thoughts to heal them.

When the AIDS crisis broke out in the 1980s, Louise really stepped into her ability to bring change to the world. It started when she received a phone call from someone who had AIDS and had nowhere to turn. No one knew how to help them. So Louise started a group at her home and did what she'd always done – spoke about love and invited anyone who had anything positive to share to share it. Before she knew it, she was hosting meetings in a football field because so many people were coming out to hear her loving wisdom.

Louise was a catalyst for huge change and her book *You Can Heal Your Life* went on to sell over 50 million copies. It's my no.1 book recommendation. It has changed many lives and was the foundation for Hay House Publishers, which has become a powerful platform for spiritual teachers and authors like me to share their sacred work.

What I have come to see is that the light warriors who have gone before us all have something in common, and it's the work they do *within*. Light warriorship may require action, but it also requires a deep internal connection and devotion to love.

Light warriors not only stand up for what they believe in, they also trust that a higher power (whatever they may call it) is helping them, guiding them towards the changes they feel inspired to create.

These changes take many forms, as do the warriors themselves. Here are some of my names for light warriors who perform specialist roles, along with a quick look at what they do.

Peacekeepers

It's no surprise to learn that these warriors do their best to bring peace to their homes, families, communities and workplaces, at times to their own detriment. These amazing people need to be supported and to find their internal warrior, because they can become incredible leaders of love.

Some of them may work behind the scenes. Examples of this would be staff who work for world leaders but don't share their belligerent stance and who work quietly in the background to ease situations and find diplomatic solutions.

Change Agents

Change agents are the amazing people who lovingly inspire change in others, often based on their own healing journey. They just want to make a positive difference to others, because helping others feels like food for their soul.

An example of a change agent would be a sponsor in Alcoholics Anonymous who has been through the 12-step programme and is now lovingly guiding others through it. Or someone who was once imprisoned and is now is a counsellor to those who are behind bars.

Miracle Makers

These souls are ones who demonstrate the power of love and kindness everywhere they go – which can make real miracles!

I think the Dalai Lama is a great example, because even though his people have lost their country, temples and even lives, he goes around the world trying to inspire kindness rather than seek retribution. My prayer is that the good karma he has created will bless all the people involved in this situation and lead to the miracle of peace.

Miracle makers aren't always high profile, though. A colleague at work or a lady sitting next to you on the bus could easily be one. How would you know? Miracle makers are dedicated to *love*. It's who they are and it's all they share.

Undercover Lightworkers

This group of badasses with good-asses are my favourite. They're the ones who are out there on the front line, trying to inspire international corporations, Big Pharma, Big Oil and so on to act in a more ethical manner. They might work for companies we don't all support and carry out policies we don't all agree with, but if they weren't in place maybe worse things would happen. By being where they are they may be able to bring about meaningful shifts that contribute to healing the world.

I know one person who has been criticized because of the company they're working for, but if people could see beyond their own opinion, they'd see that they're helping so many people from the inside through charity and community outreach. We must stay open to the miraculous!

Choosing the Warrior Path

Right now, all over the world, there are many unrecognized spiritual leaders, light warriors and change bringers. We need them more than ever. We need to *become* them more than ever. There is enough room for us all and we need to rise up.

If you feel that call to make a difference, to bring change, to bring light, then this is your time.

You've probably already acted as a light warrior in your day-to-day life without even realizing it. How?

Just the other day I was driving to the gym when I felt a tug to take a different route from normal. It was pouring with rain and I saw a police car three cars ahead of me, so I was driving a little more slowly than normal(!), when for some reason my gaze was directed to the pavement and there she was – a little lady had slipped over in the rain. Her shopping bags were everywhere and she was face down, covered in blood.

The three cars in front didn't stop (including the police), but I did.

I introduced myself straight away and wanted her to feel safe because, let's be honest, I'm a six-foot guy with a big car. I asked her how long she'd been down for and she said about 10 minutes and no one had noticed her.

I was able to help her get home, get cleaned up and get her husband home early. He was so pleased I'd got her home safely and since I've heard she's doing well.

Stepping onto the warrior path can be as simple as helping someone who needs it. It's about 'doing the right thing'. It's also about standing strong with someone who needs it. It's about showing fierce love.

Here are some other examples of stepping into light warriorship:

- Standing up for someone who's being bullied at work, at school or in the street.
- Speaking to someone you know no one else is speaking to (I've heard this can even save lives).
- Performing a random act of kindness.
- Standing up for an animal you know is being mistreated.
- Stopping someone from doing something that you know will cause harm or distress to others.
- Stepping in and splitting up a fight.
- Helping someone who's being racially targeted.

Let's get this clear, though: being a light warrior doesn't mean you're running around getting involved in altercations wherever you go. It's essentially a peaceful path – it's about standing in the light and choosing not to be moved from it.

A light warrior also chooses to become a light that inspires change, a light that serves, inspires and loves. They reclaim the space that is rightfully theirs, meaning they don't get pulled down by the drama or the expectations of those around them, but let their light shine out. They choose to be a force of love rather than be pulled into their own worst nightmare by fear. They know they are connected to love – they are ready to look into their own eyes and see the awesome presence of love shining behind them.

I suppose you could say being a light warrior is essentially being a lightworker, only with a black belt in bad-assery. It's choosing to be fierce, strong and fiery – with a huge serving of love!

The True Warrior

I've had a deep calling to serve since I was very young – a desire to be a support, inspiration and guide to others. I've always had great empathy for others, particularly those who have been pulled into the deep dark hole of their own fear. I believe in supporting people and serving as an example to show that anything is possible.

Over the last few years, I've experienced some harsh criticism. People have claimed I'm 'not spiritual enough' and asked how I dare teach people about raising their vibration while still using swear words or, even worse, *drinking coffee*. (Don't even dare try to come between me and my latte!) People have said to me (shock alert) that having an alcoholic beverage can 'take us away from spirit'.

Don't worry – that's just not true. Here's what I've learned: we can't *not* be spiritual, simply because *we are spirit*. It's who we are. Sure, we can either deny our spiritual roots or develop our spiritual practice, but we are spirit and that's that. (Gin and tonic for me, thanks.)

Vibration is important, though. So I get where these critics are coming from. When we align ourselves with a lower vibration or a word that doesn't seem 'high vibe', we can lower our frequency (become less aware of our spiritual nature), but what if – *what if* – we *didn't* see any of those practices as low vibe? Would they have the same effect then?

The point I'm making is that being a warrior is about developing *your own spiritual connection* and doing what feels right *for you*. It's about doing what honours your own sense of worth.

Basically, being a light warrior is about being yourself. Being true to yourself. Being authentic. It's about moving to a place of self-acceptance, because through accepting yourself you are energetically bringing acceptance into the world. It's not about looking spiritual or appearing spiritual or running off to join some ashram tucked away in the Himalayas (trust me, I've done it for us all), it's about lighting up wherever you are now, however you are now, and realizing all that you are doing internally, on a spiritual level, is also serving the world. What you do for yourself on the inside is ultimately what you are offering up on the outside.

So, being a light warrior is about finding the balance between give and take. It's about making sure that you have enough energy, love and focus to go out there and serve to the best of your ability. If swearing helps you do that, fine. Warriors aren't here to adhere to the rules of other people's egos or expectations, they're here to follow the light of their soul and serve the world in a way that also serves them.

Your vision of spiritual and my vision of spiritual may be different, but the true heart of a warrior embraces this entirely.

Are you ready to awaken your warrior heart?

Chapter 2

AWAKENING THE WARRIOR HEART

*'Listen to the wind - it talks. Listen to the silence
- it speaks. Listen to your heart - it knows.'*
NATIVE AMERICAN PROVERB

The heart is a sacred space. Physically, it's the organ that pumps blood around our body, keeping oxygen moving through our cells and keeping us alive. Energetically, it's the space that allows us to give and receive love. Both energetically and physically, the heart space can expand and contract. To awaken the heart of the warrior is to consciously choose expansion.

In most spiritual traditions, there's a tale of a spiritual warrior. Usually these souls are both in communication with a higher source and in a battle with their biggest fear. They are led by love, by purpose, devotion and conviction. They are brave beings who want nothing more than happiness for their people and all those connected to them.

My favourite warrior story is of the Hindu monkey god Hanuman:

Hanuman was the protector of Lord Rama and his consort, Sita, and head of their army. The story goes that he brought their kingdom through a war. When it was over, a celebratory procession took place, with many dancers and performers entertaining all who were there.

Hanuman approached the throne of the great god and goddess and knelt down, tilting his head forward as if to receive a reward.

Rama went over and embraced him, saying that he could never repay him for his kind acts and dedication. Sita, however, felt she needed to honour him in a more physical way and proceeded to take off her favourite pearl necklace and place it around his neck.

Hanuman looked down at the pearls and began to bite them open one by one and peer inside them.

Sita was shocked. 'What are you doing, Hanuman? Those are precious pearls that I have given you to honour your courage.'

Hanuman said, 'I am looking for you and Lord Rama inside them. If you aren't there, the gift will be worthless.'

Sita was bemused by what she heard. She looked at Rama for support.

Hanuman went on, 'All I want in this world is your love. I love you both so much that if I were to rip open my chest and reveal my heart, your image would be there.'

Lord Rama and Sita were touched by Hanuman's sentiments, then amazed when he began to rip open his chest, layer by layer of skin, flesh and muscle, to reveal his heart.

And there they were: an image of Lord Rama and his goddess, Sita, sitting on their thrones was imprinted on Hanuman's heart.

This story is powerful and enlightening. It reminds us that no matter how we see the divine or what we call it, it will always be anchored in our heart.

To awaken the warrior heart is to remember that we have this inner spark, this internal connection to the divine, the universal life-force, the cosmic presence that runs through all that is and ever will be. It is light in presence and love in essence. It is what a scientist will call 'the quantum field' and a Spiritualist will call 'spirit'. It is intelligent beyond our human understanding, but it will show itself to us in a way that we will understand. To Hanuman, it appeared as a goddess and god. To you, it may appear different. However you see the divine is perfect. Just know it is wholly loving and wholly accepting.

The divine waits gently in the heart of the warrior.

Awakening the heart of the warrior is taking the opportunity to really drop back into the heart space and check in with that love that will never cease to be. My friend Meggan Watterson describes it as 'the love that is love that is love', and she's right. This love, this presence, this essence is so in love with us that our human mind can't even comprehend the depth of that love.

We are loved.

We are so loved, but the truth is that most of the time we forget this. Through our beliefs and thoughts we create another reality.

Now I'm not meaning to trip you out here, but I do want to bring you to the awareness that the world we see around us is in fact illusionary. We're kind of in *The Matrix*. The world we experience is an expression of the 'truths' we believe in. It's also a by-product of what our parents, peers and ancestors have believed. Everything we know on a human level has been passed on, but when we step back into the true warrior essence within, we choose our own experience.

And that means *you*. You have the capacity to awaken from a fear-based dream to a love-based reality. You have the capacity to reconnect with the love within on a daily basis. You can make this your spiritual practice. Your focus. Your reality. It *is* reality. As one of my main spiritual references, *A Course in Miracles*, says, 'Only love is real.'

Allow the divine love in your heart to be your compass as you step onto your light warrior path.

✕ *Warrior Heart Prayer*

Divine presence,

I am ready to know you like never before.

Like a spark of light within my heart.

I give you permission to lead the way.

Spend some time just breathing and becoming aware of what this prayer really means to you. You are remembering and strengthening your sacred bond with the divine. This is a very exciting and special time.

There is a good chance that you may receive inspiration or guidance. *A Course in Miracles* describes 'inspiration' as 'a result of genuine devotion'. This means when you devote time to connecting with the divine within, it is inevitable you will receive a download of information. You may unlock this instantly or it may be revealed over time.

What If Your Heart Could Never Be Broken?

'The wound is where the light enters.'
RUMI

I'm fascinated by the science and philosophy of yoga, a gift to the world that has been handed down through Sanskrit texts that are over 5,000 years old. Within these texts is information on the chakras, the energy centres of the body. I've written about them in my previous books. The one chakra I want to write about now is the heart.

The heart chakra is known in Sanskrit as *Anahata*, a word that means 'unstruck' or essentially 'unbroken'. All those years ago the masters who created yoga were onto something incredibly important – that the heart *cannot* be broken.

Now, before heart surgeons start writing in, sure, we know the organ can break down, but right now we're speaking about the spiritual heart, the part within us that represents our soul, our true self, the essence that will survive when the body dies, the part of us that will move back to the oneness of life, or what I like to call 'spirit'.

To understand this, you may want to call your heart centre your 'higher heart'. It's the energetic vortex within you that connects you to love. I like to imagine it as a nebula within us that can feed us wisdom if we open up to it. And the ancient yogis knew that this was an energy that would never disperse or fade away.

So, when we are faced with 'heartbreak', it's not a real experience. No, seriously. It feels real, it feels scary and it feels lonely. But the truth is it's not our *heart* that's breaking, it's our *ego*. Our plans haven't worked out and we feel that we've been separated from what we want – a person, a situation, our health, even our power. But, according to physics, everything exists within everything – we are part of the energy that contains all that is. We are united with it. Therefore it's not possible to be separated from anyone, anything, or even love itself.

Now this isn't to say you aren't going to have the experience of heartache or feel as though your heart is broken. And you have every right to feel – never let anyone take that away from you. Emotions are like angels – they come with powerful messages. But once you have acknowledged how you feel, accept the message and move on. That's when the real work begins.

I know that many of you will question this, because you've heard of, or may even know of, people dying 'from a broken heart'. I know it has happened. So it's important to say that the heart I'm speaking about here is the *energetic* heart. I believe that if we can understand that energy, it can help us get over great suffering in life, but some of us are not ready to do so and I respect that.

As a warrior, you're going to experience wounds. If you think about the warriors who have gone before us, you'll remember that they've all experienced trials and tribulations. They've had to find ways of healing their wounds and then moving on from them. You must do this too. We all must. It's not easy, but it can be done.

The remedy that will allow you to begin healing a 'broken' heart is the knowledge that the higher heart is actually your truest and highest self and is therefore whole, healed and complete – as are you. Your heart is not broken – it's just a feeling. Hold on to this thought. Let it be your knight in shining armour.

Reminding yourself that you are always connected and interconnected with everyone and everything you love will give you much comfort. Just moving into that idea will help. Even though you may feel separate in some way, it is far from the truth.

Connecting with the Heart

Recently, while presenting my Hay House radio show, I received a call from a listener who had experienced a lot of heartache in her life. She had been hurt, abused and let down by family members, partners and even colleagues, and had gone through what she could only describe as 'many dark nights'.

During our call she explained that through her belief in angels and willingness to forgive, she was now feeling a freedom she had never imagined possible. But there was one challenge – how could she open her heart again?

I closed my eyes and connected with her angels. The message was loud and clear: 'The greatest illusion in this situation is the idea that the heart can be closed. It is not possible.'

I relayed the message. Word for word.

And then my intuition kicked in. I added, 'You've been convinced that because you've been hurt and find it difficult to trust, your heart is closed. But this isn't real. Your heart is the most whole aspect of who you are. It's open, and it's everything else that's closed, including your mind. Your past experiences of betrayal and hurt have made you feel that it's not possible to open your heart again and so you're creating an illusionary experience where people won't see you, acknowledge you or give you the loving respect you deserve.'

The caller began to cry. She felt the resonance of the message. It touched her because it was true. Her heart was open, only her mind was shut. She couldn't accept the possibility of being loved unconditionally and so was experiencing a major sense of disconnection.

Sometimes the challenge we think we're facing is actually a mental barrier rather than an energetic trauma that we think has halted our experience of love. Through deep spiritual practice we can access the warrior within and light up whatever darkness we face.

Heart-Connecting Practices

Your heart is already open, but, like my radio show caller, you may be facing the illusion that it is shut down. The more time you spend connecting with your heart centre, the more these illusionary barriers will fade away and you'll be able to 'feel into' its open energy. I often place my hands on my heart and just breathe into this space to connect with the loving presence within.

The miracles that lie within the heart space can ultimately only be felt, and it is of vital importance that you constantly develop your ability to feel in order to anchor yourself in this deep love. Here are a few practices you might like to try.

➤——— Ujjayi Breathing ◄———

Ujjayi is a Sanskrit word that means 'victorious' and Ujjayi breathing is a breathing technique, a *pranayama*, used in many yoga practices to generate energy and create heat within the body. It brings more energy because it increases oxygen in the body, yet it slows down the breathing. Its rhythmic motion is reassuring and so it is able to help you relax and become present. It's simple, effective and an incredible tool for any light warrior who just needs a moment to gather their energy and their thoughts.

If it is practised during exercise, it will help build up heat in the body so that you sweat out any impurities, and so on an energetic level it also has a detoxifying effect.

It's extremely powerful when you're anxious. The breath switches on and becomes a little remedy to keep you warm, fuzzy and calm.

It is known as 'ocean breath' because it sounds like the waves washing onto the shore. The sound is created by contracting the glottis (the opening between the vocal cords) at the back of the throat. Then, as you breathe in and out, the air creates a rushing sound.

- Sitting in a comfortable position with your spine upright (maybe on the floor against the wall) or in a chair, bring your hands onto your belly.

- Contract the back of your throat (gently) and begin to breathe deeply through your nostrils. Breathing towards your hands (filling your belly), observe the sound your throat is creating. It should sound like a gentle ocean wave.

- Exhale with the same contraction in the throat for the same amount of time you inhaled.

Use this as a meditation or to strengthen any existing meditation practice.

If you practise Ujjayi breathing while walking (you don't need to use your hands) or driving, it will eventually become a valuable aid on your light warrior pathway.

Open Heart Prayer

Dear universe,

Thank you for reminding me of the splendour of my heart.

It feels so good to know that my capacity to love and be loved is open. Thank you, thank you, thank you. It feels so good.

Today I choose to share the universe's love through my energy and my smile.

Meditating on the Divine

We all see the divine differently. Just as Hanuman opened up his chest to reveal his image of the divine within, we all also have the capacity to delve deep inside to see how the divine is for us.

I don't know about you, but I'm a really visual person. I have to see things to really get an idea of them. You know when a friend tries to describe a piece of clothing over the phone and you can't make up your mind about it until you've seen it?

When I delved deep into meditation to see the divine within my heart, I actually saw a heart – a gigantic heart suspended in a sky filled with stars. And every time it beat, the beat became an angel.

As crazy as it seems, this image gave me such a powerful insight into my spiritual connection. For the last 13 years or so I'd dedicated my life to understanding angels and their connection with us and the universe, and here it was, right in front of my eyes.

Angels are the heartbeat of the divine.

That image reinforced for me that angels are not separate from the divine – they are one. Therefore, when I commune with angels, I connect directly with the divine.

This was so reassuring for me. This image was something to remember, to see again and again, to visualize, connect with and feel safe within.

This isn't to place ideas in your head or encourage you to see the divine this way. But my prayer is that by exploring your sacred connection, you'll see an image that will support your growth.

If you already have an idea of how the divine seems to you – maybe you call it God or Goddess – then you can just spend some time consciously connecting to it. If not, try this meditation. It may just bring you that depth of connection that you need.

➤➤➤ ➝ The Hanuman Meditation ⬅ ⬸⬸

In this meditation I encourage you to call in the energy of Hanuman. Take a moment to google image him and see the beautiful icons that have been created of him. That will give you something to work with. Let this incredible warrior be your guide as you remove any barriers that block your way into the heart space where the divine resides.

If, however, this doesn't feel right for you, call in any spirit guide, angel, saint or loved one you trust to guide you.

Top Tip: With longer guided meditations I recommend recording the steps for yourself using your mobile phone's voice recorder or similar, so that you don't have to Zen with one eye open.

- Start by setting your intention and offering up a prayer:

  Hanuman, warrior heart, thank you for being my guide today. I am now ready to delve deep into the cave of my heart and see my personal image of the divine.

  I am thrilled to connect with this deeper part of myself.

  Thank you for supporting me in this internal discovery.

  I welcome your light, like a blazing torch, to lead me.

  And so together we go into the heart!

- Turn on your deepest Ujjayi breathing (*see page 21*).

- Focus directly on your heart region. Feel your chest expanding and contracting with each and every breath.

- Imagine a bright light in the centre of your chest. Each time you exhale, allow this light to grow brighter and brighter.

- Allow this light to expand. Feel yourself being drawn in by it.

- Deeper and deeper, layer by layer, feel yourself being drawn into the divine matrix of your heart.

- Feel ready. Feel willing. Be open.

- Allow yourself to become aware of the divine presence within you. Allow it to be revealed.

- Spend as much time in receiving mode as you need. Maybe even have a conversation or dialogue with the expression of the divine that is revealed to you.

- When you are ready, make your way back to the room.

- Give thanks to your guide, give thanks to the divine and feel cherished.

Warrior Workout

Your opportunity to step into your warrior self begins here. Here are some suggestions for igniting this incredible energy within you *now*:

~ Send loving thoughts to someone you know who is in need.

~ Send loving thoughts to someone who has previously challenged you – they need it most.

~ Practise yoga and in particular spend time on heart-opening poses. If you're new to yoga, speak to your local studio and tell them this is what you're working on – they'll know exactly which poses to guide you through. If you like, book a private lesson. If you're already a yogi, it's all back-bending poses, camel, wheel, updog and so on.

~ If you do any energy healing, aim the energy directly into your heart chakra.

~ Dance to your favourite music and spend time loving life.

~ Every time you are about to say you hate something, say three to five things you *love* instead.

Chapter 3
LETTING THE SHIELDS DOWN

'Our spirit is the true shield.'
MORIHEI UESHIBA, FOUNDER OF AIKIDO

Though I grew up having psychic experiences, I never once considered the idea that one day I would be able to develop a relationship with angels – to commune directly with heaven. I went to Sunday school and Boys' Brigade, and with these strong Christian influences in my life, I learned that heaven was another place, somewhere you couldn't touch unless it was your time to go there.

On discovering angels as a teenager, I was mesmerized by the idea that everyone had a guardian angel – that no one had been forgotten. I was thrilled to learn that our angel stayed with us through our many lifetimes.

I remember reading angel books and learning that we all had the ability to connect with angels, but even though I tried, I could never have the experiences that were described in the books. Why? It bothered me. I needed to understand angels from a personal space.

I upped my meditation practice, even though I was a teenager finding my way, and it seemed the more I did, the more I had a need for integrity. That word 'integrity' is sexy. Its meaning is even sexier: 'honesty; fairness; having strong moral principles that you refuse to change'.

Being honest and fair, going with the heart and doing what feels right are so important to me – and are key to being a light warrior. And eventually I discovered that trying to have someone else's spiritual experience wasn't the way forward. I had to wait for my own.

We cannot have someone else's spiritual experience. We must have our own.

Finally, one day I saw an angel. I'll never forget that moment. There it was – a glorious being made of light, almost seven feet tall, standing there. Eyes as dark as the midnight sky gazing lovingly into my own... There was nothing this angel could not see. It knew everything about me. My whole history. My secrets. I was essentially naked.

The only way I can describe the feeling is that it was like being reborn. Or how you feel the first time someone you've fallen in love with sees you naked. It was real, raw and honest.

That got me thinking. In this world, so many of us have been programmed into thinking that we're going to be hurt. We have the idea that someone can hurt us, break our heart or let us down. It's almost as though we're encouraged to prepare for the worst or live behind what I can only describe a shield.

You've encountered these shields. You know the energy that you can feel between you and someone you find it difficult to get through to? Or the feeling when you're speaking to someone and you're not getting a warm response? Or any response? That's a shield. Some people call them brick walls. The truth is, you've probably got some up.

These shields can be up unconsciously and sometimes consciously too. I know I put mine up a lot and I have to work really hard to bring them down.

The shields that I'm speaking about are *not* psychic protection (we'll speak about this later), they are emotionally numbing shields that block our light from getting out and being seen.

When we put them up, we step into a mindset of 'nothing can hurt me now' and believe we're protected, but that's not true. The truth is that because we've accepted we can get hurt in the first place, that's exactly what we've put into our vibration and exactly what we'll attract.

It's down to the law of attraction. This spiritual law will work even when we're not intending to use it. The basis of it is that like attracts like. Everything is essentially a magnet and what we give off is what we attract. So if we're putting up a defensive shield, we'll attract experiences in which we need to be defensive.

Defensive shields can leave us *powerless* rather than powerful.

The good news is that when we change our thoughts, intentions, reactions and therefore energy, we change our experiences.

Choosing to Drop the Shields

So many people ask me how they can have more spiritual experiences. My answer is always changing. But when I look back at my initial angelic experience, I remember that my shields dropped instantly. The angel could see everything. I feel this happened because I was so ready to see angels and trusted them so much.

There's a quote from *A Course in Miracles* that blows my mind and I constantly refer to it in my meditations and daily life. It says:

> *Your task is not to seek for love, but merely*
> *to seek and find all the barriers within*
> *yourself that you have built against it.*

Angels are beings of love. Spiritual experiences are expressions of love. Feeling connected to our inner warrior is about experiencing love. It's all down to love – the love that's already here and always will be. When we put up shields, we're creating barriers between ourselves and that love.

So, to have more spiritual experiences, choose to drop your shields. Choose to bring them down so that you can let love (and light) in and out freely and openly.

When it comes to angelic experiences, here's a thought: what if they aren't about seeing angels, but more about allowing angels to see us? Drop your shields and let the angels see your glory. Celebrate it with them!

On a one-day angel workshop recently I discussed the importance of dropping the shields and allowing the true self to be seen. I decided that I would lead an exercise in which we would willingly choose to drop our shields.

I encouraged the class to remind themselves that they were safe and could allow their need to protect themselves from others' judgement to fade away. Then I led them through a visualization in which all their shields dropped down.

It wasn't always easy for them – one lady said her energy field was like Fort Knox, with lots of chains, padlocks and everything you can imagine preventing anything from getting in – but many people said that they could see barriers falling.

Once the shields were down, I encouraged the group to partner up and lovingly gaze into each other's eyes, heart and ultimately soul. When I said this, I could hear giggles, see people crossing their arms and sense many stepping back. It was all too much.

I know this exercise is intense, because I've done it. It's hard to allow yourself to really be seen. We've grown so used to living in an invisible force field that we feel is going to protect us from harm but ultimately blocks out so many loving people and experiences.

Nevertheless, some of the class went ahead with the exercise. Then we broke for lunch.

After the lunch break I was approached by an attendee who wanted to have a private word. She mentioned that her family had been going through some challenges, in particular with a family member who had also been at the workshop. They had been partnered in the gazing exercise.

She said it was the first time in years that she'd been able to look into that woman's eyes and have her look into hers. She said when she'd done so, she'd been able to recognize where the pain was, where the discomfort was, and to feel compassion for the other woman. They'd gone out together for lunch and had been able to see each other like never before. It really was as if all the barriers between them had fallen.

I smiled and asked, 'Who had the barriers up then?'

She replied, 'Both of us. I thought it was just her, but then I realized I had mine up too. It felt great to bring them down.'

Most of us have barriers up against someone in our life. Most of the time it's someone we really love. And when we feel that someone's putting barriers up against us, we're probably putting barriers up against them!

As light warriors, we have to get into the driving seat of love and demonstrate what it's like to let our shields down. Ultimately, others will do the same, especially those we care about, even if they're not into spiritual development.

**We have to do what we expect from
others. Let your light lead the way.**

The Question of Power

When we're putting up shields to defend ourselves from someone or something, or even somewhere, we're ultimately saying that person, thing or place is more powerful than we are. It's almost as if we're saying that this energy, whatever it may be, is up against us and can strip us down, hurt us or make us weak. This is an illusion.

Asking Why

- Take a moment to figure out when you're putting your shields up. Why is this response happening? Who or what is involved? Is it because of something that's happened in the past? Is it because you've learned something from an external source? It could be the result of a difficult situation in your childhood or an abusive relationship. Maybe in your past these shields were pivotal to your survival. Maybe they helped you protect yourself from pain, hurt and being let down.

  Remember, the shields that we're speaking about here aren't shields of psychic protection (there's a chapter on this later), they're shields that have been created by a fear-based response to a fear-based experience. Maybe you've had to use them to get through a difficult time. Now they're probably redundant. You just haven't realized it yet.

  It's important at this stage on your warrior journey to decide to shift your point of attraction – to take the law of attraction into your own hands and use your energy and intentions to move forward.

  Check in with your heart as to why you're giving something else – whatever it is – such negative power over you.

- Take a moment to meditate on this. Just ask these questions. Feel the feelings that come up.

- And then make a note, in your journal if you have one, about your responses, because once you've worked out why you feel a certain way, you have something to work with.

When the shields drop, the light warrior is revealed.

Making the decision to drop your shields and let love in can open up your life in an amazing way.

Just the other day I was doing a coaching session with a lady called Sarah, who wanted to have more clarity on her life and her goals.

She was a real people person who also had a love for the animal kingdom. She had a dream of rescuing horses and giving them a space where they could roam wild and free without ever needing to be ridden or saddled again. Then people could come and see them and receive the benefits of horse medicine. That way she could combine her love for animals with her love for people and her desire to perform natural healing to make a difference in the world.

There are said to be many health benefits from spending time with horses, particularly mental health benefits. In fact it has become a widely recognized form of rehabilitation and therapy. And in animal medicine, the horse represents freedom. I sensed Sarah was seeking this freedom for herself.

'So what's stopping this dream from coming true then?' I asked her.

'Well, the truth is, Kyle,' she admitted, 'I prefer just to keep myself to myself and live with my animals.'

'Go on,' I encouraged. She was revealing something very important.

'Well, most people are so self-centred – they're just interested in themselves and couldn't care less about anyone else. It really annoys me, to be honest.'

It seemed that Sarah had felt misused and mistreated in the past and in some way had decided to switch herself off from the world. She didn't realize it, but her belief that most people were self-centred was actually a fear-based shield that was attracting experiences in which people behaved that way.

I explained to her that she was a wonderfully sensitive person and encouraged her to see that what she believed wasn't entirely true. Of course there are challenging and difficult people out there in the world, but there are wonderful people too.

I suggested to Sarah that if she were to drop this shield, this old way of thinking, she would have a completely different experience of life.

She thought about it, then said it made so much sense and that she was ready to experience the good in others again. I coached her through dropping her shields and asked her to get in touch again later to let me know how she was getting on.

Only a few days later I received a loving and positive email from Sarah. She told me that she had begun to change *the way she thought about the world and every day she was imagining that her shields were dropping and that the love she had inside was being reflected back to her. Best of all, only a day after seeing me she'd been introduced to a lady who was doing similar work to her dream and who lived a matter of minutes away.*

I got 'angel bumps' all over my skin when I heard about this miraculous shift that was taking Sarah closer to realizing her goal!

When we move into shield mode, it means that we are making no space for the miraculous to be present. When we drop our shields, there's room for so many opportunities!

In order to drop our shields, we have to eradicate the patterns that have led us to take on the idea that we're going to be broken or hurt. For a start, we have to stop being so defensive.

Let Go of the Need for Defence

In Lesson 153 of the *Course in Miracles* workbook, it says: 'Defencelessness is strength.' And for good reason. It's teaching us something so important. When we move into a state of defence, it means our fear is running the show. When we choose to be defenceless, we are allowing the love source within us to lead.

Where are you being defensive? Is it towards a person? Could you encourage a loving conversation with them instead? If you are constantly living in defence mode with one particular person, is it because you have grown used to bad behaviour?

Or maybe you are defensive about a certain aspect of your life. Maybe your defensiveness is actually a call for change. What is it that needs to change?

I feel it is important that the light warrior in me steps up at this point and admits that making changes may not be easy. There are going to be many people living behind these kinds of shields because it is the only way to survive. I'm thinking about those in war-torn countries and other violent situations. I don't want to come along and seem arrogant by giving a 'psychic solution' to what is a very tangible problem. I appreciate that some situations are extremely difficult and it may seem as though our efforts cannot possibly bring a solution. However, I feel it is important for as many of us as possible to do the inner work, because, as many spiritual teachers say, it *will* eventually be reflected on the outside.

So, even if we can't bring about the changes we want right now, let us do what we can on the inside and hope that the subtle shifts we create through spiritual practice, prayer, meditation and internal commitment usher angels of the greatest peace towards places where there is war, hunger and fear. May the lives of the people in those places be lifted by the internal effort we create.

When I think about world issues and feel helpless, I think about a quote from Thích Nhất Hạnh: 'The Earth will be safe when we feel safe.'

In order to feel safe, we need to surrender our need for defence. It may sound counter-intuitive, but it will change our energy and ultimately our whole environment for the better. That's the goal.

We might continue to need our shields from time to time, or slip up and move back into defensiveness for a while. If so, it doesn't mean we've failed in our mission. We should just continue on with the intention of changing. We may not think that makes a difference, but it does. And even a 'small' difference could actually be huge.

This reminds me of what I shared earlier about Gandhi. He was one man who changed himself in order to help change the world. He was just a normal young lawyer from India who began working on himself, changing his actions, changing his thinking, changing his life, and eventually he went on to become the Mahātmā, the 'great soul', who led 400 million Indians to independence. He claimed his approach was nothing new: 'Truth and nonviolence are as old as the hills. All I have done is to try experiments in both on as vast a scale as I could do.' We can use his story as inspiration to bring about changes in our own world.

✕ Surrendering the Need for Defence Prayer

Dear universe,

I hand over to you all my needs for defence.

I choose to remember that I am safe.

Thank you for reminding me of this truth.

Get Rid of Venom

Part of feeling ready to drop our shields and step out as a light warrior is getting rid of any toxic energy, or venom, that has built up inside us.

We all have acid in our belly – we need it to digest our food. In the chakra system, the belly is the fire centre of the body. It represents our will, our passions and so also our anger. Both energetically and physically, we can build up the fire/acid in our belly, something I like to call our venom.

When we're fully expressing our feelings, channelling our passions and expressing our creativity, our venom doesn't build up so much. If, however, we're not expressing ourselves, it can build up and up and become toxic energy that begins to eat away at our inspiration.

We can choose to release this toxic energy through a number of practices. These can have a freeing effect both psychically and physically. I can vouch for this because I'm quite a venomous person. Although my creative fire and juices are constantly working (and overworking), I also get pretty frustrated by the number of things I end up doing or the amount of pressure that lands on my shoulders.

One of the things I've found to be beneficial in overcoming my venom has been going for martial arts lessons. I recently took up Brazilian Jiu-Jitsu and it's been so good for physical release.

Another thing that I've done is go for private sessions with my trainer where I'll put on my boxing gloves and get all of my frustrations out by punching a bag. The relief is *incredible* and *indescribable*, so much so that I've begun recommending it to my personal coaching clients. They, too, have found it brings them a lot of relief.

There are some huge benefits to getting rid of venom. Many people I know who have had tummy issues have found themselves much better as a result, while others have spoken about an increase in creative inspiration and/or a knot of frustration in their tummy disappearing for good.

Releasing venom makes space for the miraculous.

I believe when we release the venom within, we cultivate a space where we can generate more miracles and receive more guidance and inspiration.

It's also a space for forgiveness to enter. Forgiveness is an organic energy of spirit. It occurs naturally. It isn't about letting someone get away with bad behaviour, or forgetting about bad choices we ourselves have made, it's about no longer choosing to be affected by something in the past or by someone else's fear. Forgiveness is about choosing our own spirit over fear.

Suggestions to Help You Let Go of Venom

There are many ways to release venom:

- Roll up a pillow in a duvet and punch it.

- Take up some powerful physical activity that will allow you to express your competitive spirit.

- Have a private session with a trainer – ideally using a punch bag!

- Go somewhere in nature and scream at the top of your lungs.

- If something's been bothering you, get it off your chest.

- Take a roaring venom breath (*see below*).

≫⟶ Roaring Venom Breath ⟵≪

Roaring venom breath is actually an adaption of a technique I learned on my spiritual quest in India. When I was studying Kriya yoga in southern India, we did a pose called cobra, which is fairly common. However, in most yoga classes, cobra pose is used to inhale, whereas in this particular tradition it was used to exhale – and to exhale with great force. The idea was that if we were doing the pose with a 'roaring breath', on an energetic level we would be expelling all the venom that could hold us back. This idea stuck with me and so I began to roar my venom out whenever I could feel it building. I called this 'roaring venom breath'.

Roaring venom breath is easy, but I urge you to do it in a safe space or where no one can hear you, especially if you are easily embarrassed. I have given my cats a fright way too many times while doing this technique, so do also take any sleeping pets or babies into consideration.

All you have to do is stick out your tongue like a snake and expel all your energetic venom via a roaring sound or, if you prefer, a hissing sound (for more specifics, *see below*). Either way, I find the louder, the better. That way you can really get a release – it's like screaming at the top of your lungs on the top of a hill.

When do you do it? Whenever something begins to make your blood boil or you can feel venom building up inside, it's time for a roaring breath.

How do you do it?

- Exhale completely, then close your eyes and take a massive Ujjayi breath, that is, contract the back of your throat and breathe in deeply through your nostrils.

- Hold your breath and imagine all your venom preparing to be expelled.

- Open your eyes, open your mouth, stick out your tongue and *roar*.

- Do this three to five times or as many times as you feel is necessary.

I often do this in the car when I'm on the motorway. Don't worry – I just keep my eyes open through the whole process. Give it a whirl.

Finally... Drop the Shields

Now you have chosen to let your fear-based shields down, understood why they were there in the first place, surrendered the need for defence and got rid of venom, how do you actually drop the shields?

First you must take some time in meditation to remind yourself that ultimately *you are safe*. Spending time meditating on this truth will prepare your spirit to move back into the driving seat so that your ego can no longer project its plan for failure and fear into your energy field.

As for dropping the shields themselves, well, they are your shields, so you are welcome to create your own ceremony or prayer, but here are my suggestions:

Prayer to Drop Your Shields

Taking time to regularly say a prayer that drops your shields will keep you in an open space that will attract support, abundance and spiritual experiences.

I now choose to drop any shields that have been created out of fear.

I am grateful for the lessons these shields have brought me.

Today I choose to accept my personal power and claim my safety through defencelessness.

I am safe here!

And so it is!

Add your own celebration noises and dances in at the end to support the truth in your prayer. I like to howl!

⯈⯈⟶ Dropping Your Shields ⟵⯇⯇

- Sit comfortably with your hands relaxed in your lap. I recommend you have your palms facing upwards to show that you are opening your energy.

- Begin Ujjayi breathing.

- Set your intention to dissolve all the fear-based shields that are around you by stating it, either internally or out loud. Add: 'I am safe!'

- Then bring one hand to your heart and the other hand to your belly. Breathe deeply. Connect with the energy of love within you. Connect with the creative force within you.

- Call your angels and guides into the space with you. Thank them for holding the space for you to dissolve your fear-based shields.

- In your mind, imagine that the love in your heart is reaching out to your shields. See them begin to fade away or even drop instantly at the touch of true love.

- You may feel a new sense of clarity, openness and space.

- Thank your angels and guides.

Let's be realistic – your shields are going to go back up several times during your life, or even day, but you are in charge of your energy. You can command them to drop at any time.

Whenever I feel my shields going up and I know they're not going to serve me, I simply command: 'Shields, drop!' either internally or out loud, and continue with my experience.

Warrior Workout

~   In meditation, ask your guides to reveal where in your life you could have a shield of fear.

~   Take time to study your behaviour in that area, especially in situations that make you uncomfortable, and vow to work on dropping those shields.

~   Practise the roaring venom breath to release any old energy that may be stagnant around you.

~   Work with a partner and discuss where you feel your shields could be dropped.

~   Work through the 'Dropping Your Shields' process and take note of any shifts you feel.

Chapter 4
WARRIOR GUIDES

'These bodies are perishable, but the dwellers in these bodies are eternal, indestructible and impenetrable.'
BHAGAVAD GITA

The path of a light warrior is not a solo path – it is filled with spiritual support. In order to follow this calling, we must open up to the tremendous amount of support that is being offered to us.

When I think of the great warrior stories I've heard over the years, there's always some sort of connection to the divine. St George reached out to the divine, Joan of Arc invoked Archangel Michael and Arjuna had Krishna.

Arjuna's story is told in the *Bhagavad Gita*, one of the leading texts in Hinduism. He is a powerful warrior who is in conflict both internally, as he faces a series of moral challenges, and externally, as he fights for his kingdom. During this challenging time, he turns for advice to his charioteer, Krishna, who is an embodiment of Vishnu, one of the main Hindu gods. Although Krishna doesn't make any decisions for Arjuna, he guides him through the challenges he faces.

You, too, have a spiritual support system that is available to you 24/7. It is a powerful congregation of spiritual beings who are on standby, waiting for your call. Depending on your beliefs and what feels comfortable to you, you can bring together an SOS team of support you can reach out to at any time.

I firmly believe that you can never have enough friends and never have enough guides. I have a range of beings, guides, angels and animal totems I reach out to on a daily basis and for different purposes. You may already have a wad of guides you know or are ready to know better, or maybe this is the first time you've thought of connecting. Either way, know that help is available on your light warrior path.

Guides through the Realms

Guides, angels and spiritual mentors are known in all four corners of the world. They may have different names, faces and characteristics in different traditions, but the one thing they have in common is the fact that they are representatives of love, support and protection. I'll mention just a few here to give you an idea.

The Aboriginal people of Australia believe in a variety of spiritual beings who are connected to the land and people. They believe that the elders of their tribes can contact them and channel their wisdom. They reach out to these beings for help in surviving drought, finding food and ensuring the peaceful passing of those who are ready to die. Cave paintings depict long and lanky Mimi spirits from northern Australia with large faces and halos of light, and round-faced *wandjina*, creation spirits from the Kimberley region, with large dark eyes and no mouth.

In the Shinto belief system of Japan there are spirit beings called the Kami. They are nature spirits and also the spirits of venerable ancestors. They are said to be able to move through the air as if they have wings. Folk art depicts them emerging from caves of light wearing long silk robes, with peaceful expressions on their faces.

Tibetan Buddhists gain spiritual support from beings called *bodhisattvas*. The word means 'a person whose being is perfect knowledge'. Robert Thurman, Professor of Indo-Tibetan Buddhist Studies at Colombia University, describes these beings as 'the Arch-angelic beings of Buddhism'. The story goes that the lord of compassion, Avalokiteshvara, looks upon the land and witnesses humankind going through great suffering. He cries tears of compassion and his teardrops fall and hit the mud. From the mud comes a lotus, and from the lotus the *bodhisattvas* are born. These beings then reach out to those who are suffering. They hold back from achieving enlightenment themselves so that they can guide those in need – an act of sheer compassion.

On the other side of the world, Native American people have cave paintings of angelic-like beings interacting with people. They also believe that animal guides, both in physical and spiritual form, bring messages from Great Father Sky and Mother Earth.

There are spirit helpers of one kind or another in every spiritual tradition. The Druids have guardian spirits of the land. In India they have devas and deities who are embodiments of the divine. In the Abrahamic religions (Christianity, Judaism and Islam), there are angels (*malaika* in Arabic).

For me there's no denying these beings exist, because people have always connected with them and shared knowledge of them. Now let us discover your own spiritual guidance squad and how to initiate and deepen your connection with them.

Angels

Angels are a divine race of spiritual beings who are dedicated to the healing and nurturing of the universe. They are formless, being created of divine energy, but appear as individual beings so that we can have a personal relationship with them. Ultimately, they are one with the divine.

Angels are non-human beings and it is very rare that adult humans become angels, though babies who don't make it safely to Earth, through whatever circumstance, have the opportunity to become angels and will continue to guide their family on an angelic level from the other side.

'Angel' is a Greek word that means 'messenger', and angels are messengers of the divine. They can bring important guidance.

All of us have one or more angels working with us. We all have a guardian angel, who is our protector and guide through our whole life – and beyond. Our angel has been with us through lifetimes upon lifetimes and is the record-keeper of our soul journey and expansion. They will never, ever leave us. Depending on where we are in our lives, there will be other angels helping us too. These angels can come and go.

All angels have divine intelligence and can help us when it comes to understanding where we are and how to navigate forward. Although our angel(s) cannot make decisions for us, they can be called upon to support and guide us towards the decision that best supports our needs.

Angels are ultimately warriors, even though they appear in many different forms and have very different energies. There are angels who are fiery, with a fierce love that will transmute any fear, and there are angels who are so soft and graceful that their sensitivity brings incredible healing to all the hearts that allow them in.

Archangels

The best known of the many different types of angel are the archangels. These are somewhat like the managers of the other angels. I love to imagine them all sitting round a huge table up in heaven, overseeing the goings-on of the planet.

Archangels are like gigantic pools of love and support energy that we can go to. We can invoke them as well. We can draw them down into our energy to provide a powerful armour of love, guidance and protection. In my personal meditations I have seen all of the major archangels express this warrior-like energy and take on a human-like appearance clad in the most incredible armour.

When you are moving into your light warrior energy, you can call on the archangel who best supports whatever you are working on or through and/or imagine yourself cloaked in the colour associated with that archangel. That will allow you to step into their spiritual armour and feel safe and guided at any time. You can imagine this armour moving over you before going to work, home or even before you are about to participate in meditation or other spiritual practices. Over the years I've found myself pausing in the car or even in the supermarket to invoke the angelic light armour of the archangel I know is best suited to support me.

Archangels (and angels) can be warrior guides to *all* of those who call on them, however many people that might be at any one time, because they exist in a time that is not linear or limited.

Here's a short list of archangels, their armour colour and what they can help with:

- Ariel – golden; helps with staying peaceful under pressure.

- Azrael – coral red; helps with making major life changes.

- Chamuel – ruby red; helps with overcoming barriers surrounding love.

- Gabriel – pink and white; helps with speaking truth and motherhood issues.

- Haniel – pale lilac; helps with honouring sensitivity and understanding intuition.

- Jeremiel – orange and gold; helps with moving into the safety of forgiveness.

- Jophiel – light green; helps with clearing the air and clearing anything that's cluttered.

- Metatron – magenta; helps with shifting gears to create a deeper spiritual connection.

- Michael – blue; helps with stepping into an armour of complete protection.

- Orion – midnight blue; helps with setting intentions to create the miraculous.

- Raguel – bright orange; helps with making peace and issues regarding justice.

- Raphael – emerald; helps with health, wellness and all matters of healing.

- Raziel – gold and saffron; helps with understanding spiritual laws.

- Sandalphon – copper; helps with prayer and feeling grounded.

- Uriel – bright yellow; helps with joy, energy and problem-solving.

- Zadkiel – violet; helps with matters of transformation and understanding challenges.

Don't worry if you can't remember the specific archangel for the specific issue – many people just develop a bond with an archangel they feel drawn to. I love it when this happens because it allows us to have an archangel we can turn to any time we feel the need.

Spirit Guides

Spirit guides, or just 'guides', are like angels in that they are here to guide us, but they have had human experiences too (well, most of them have).

When the body dies, the soul moves back to the heart of the universe, which is essentially what mediums refer to as 'spirit', and has the opportunity to continue serving the world. Souls who have been through many life lessons and hardships and experienced real growth in their human existence can choose to help others with similar lessons in order to help the growth of the entire world. This act of service can be an awesome support to a soul who's currently residing on Earth.

We all have one of these spirit guides, a soul who has moved back to spirit but consciously decided to guide us along the pathway of our life. Not only does this being have angelic-like service qualities, they also have life experience that allows them to offer real compassion because they know what it's like to be here.

Our guide isn't allocated to us by someone with a clipboard (although if that visual helps, then use it), but by a divine law that aligns our soul's compatibility with theirs. It's almost as though a magnetic force draws their spiritual intelligence towards us and they see the opportunity to serve, so they take it.

There are also spirit guides who will come into our life as needed and then leave, and other guides who work with the whole world. They are called ascended masters.

Building a relationship with your spirit guide is an amazing process. I remember how mine started. I was 15 and just discovering angels, spirit guides and psychic communication. I didn't do anything fancy, I just read a book on spirit guides and it gave a step-by-step meditation that asked you to imagine yourself in a golden cloak of light and your third eye chakra opening and then invite your guide to draw close. I followed the instructions and instantly I saw myself in a big house that had patterned rugs on the floor. Before me stood an old-school-style butler. He was in a suit with a dickie bow (kinda like Alfred in *Batman*) and he declared, 'My name is Jonathan. I'm your guide!'

Now you may be thinking a butler's a strange sort of guide to have. You've probably heard that nearly everyone who's into spirit guides has a monk, Native American chief or Egyptian priestess as a guide, right? Well, although these are all valid types of spirit guide, there are less exotic ones out there waiting to help us and they are just as effective.

During that meditation I was young and ignorant. I just thought, *OMG, how cool – I just met my spirit guide*, but I learned much more about things as I progressed. Now I realize that a butler is perfect as a guide, because butlers are dedicated to service – and service of the highest quality.

Jonathan has been an incredible guide to me over the years, particularly with the development of my mediumship (which is always developing). Whenever I went to my development circle and entered meditation, he would be the first person I saw. So I always felt safe and protected before delving into the unknown. And if ever I felt unsure about anything during the meditation, I would bring Jonathan's energy to mind and there he would be to serve and protect me.

Spirit guides can act as doorkeepers who filter the information that comes to you when you're working in a psychic way; they can also be protectors who keep you safe, especially when you're facing personal darkness, fear or your shadow. (More on the shadow later.)

The most amazing thing is the amount of spiritual support that is offered to all beings on Earth, and in order to receive that help, all you have to do is reach out for it.

Getting the Best from Your Guides and Angels

In order to progress along your light warrior pathway, you'll need to draw on the support of your angels, archangels and guides to suss out your fears, blocks and challenges. The path of the warrior is about truth and integrity. It's about acknowledging what's really going on, rather than what we would like to see happen.

We can reach up to our guides for help with this. We can also ask them for help with stuff we want. It's totally cool to ask them for this, but we can actually upgrade our spiritual experience by asking them for what we *need*. I found personally that my entire journey shifted when I began to ask for this.

Ask for what you need.

What I needed was guidance, understanding and insight. Who doesn't need that? Guides and angels can't make decisions for us, but they can help us understand the consequences of our actions and how to make the best choice for our growth.

Even if you're unsure about the identity of your angels and guides, don't let this hold you back from reaching out to them. The more we reach out to our guides (and when I say 'guides', I'm talking angels, spirit guides and anyone else who can help), the more space we make in our life for them to make contact.

In the previous chapter we spoke about dropping the shields that could be blocking support and abundance. Here's another way to ensure you're keeping all lines of communication open – reach out.

⟫⟶ Initiating Contact ⟵⟪

I invite you to set a five-minute timer up on your mobile phone a few times a week, or every day if you like, and move into meditation with the intention of knowing your angels and guides. Just do it for those five minutes, but do vow to sit there with that intention in mind. Begin to create a routine where you make it possible for your guides to contact you.

Keep a journal handy to jot down your feelings, any messages that come through or anything that you see.

———————————

✕ *Initiating Contact Prayers*

If you wish, you can use simple prayers to initiate contact with your guides. Here are some examples:

Dear guides, thank you for revealing to me your presence and anything that I need to know!

Hey, spirit team, my heart is wide open and I am ready to receive your guidance! Thanks for bringing it through.

Dear angels and guides, I am ready to know you like never before! Thank you for coming through in my meditation today.

Welcoming Signs and Reminders

I do love a sign – a lil' wink from my spiritual support team that makes me feel cherished and loved. Signs are a wonderful way to know that we're on the pathway of light. They often arrive without us having to ask, though we can ask if we need a little reassurance.

For a few years I've refrained from asking directly, but have made my life open and welcoming to reminders that my angels and guides are with me. The reason for this is that if you're a light warrior, you *know* your guides have your back. When you're asking for proof they exist, you're actually reducing your connection to them, because essentially you're questioning that connection. Also, I believe that through fully accepting that your guides are there for you, you become more open to communication with them, including through signs.

You can, however, call out to your guides to let them know that you welcome signs that will help you along your light warrior path. These can be especially welcome when you're unsure about a decision. They will also give you extra encouragement, because you'll be reminded that your guides are right there, cheerleading for your soul.

Many of my spiritual friends tell their guides which signs they'd like to see, whereas I prefer just to leave it wide open for reminders to come in whatever shape or form they need to.

Welcoming Sign Prayers

Thank you, angels and warrior guide squad, for reminding me of your presence through signs!

Thank you, angels and warrior guides, for sending me a [state your sign] so that I know this decision is congruent with my life purpose. I am grateful for your support!

You can ask for anything as a sign, such as a coloured feather, your favourite animal, a number sequence or type of flower.

Know that the sign may come in a different way from how you initially intended. For example, you might ask for a white dove and someone drives in front of you with a white dove number sticker on their car. Guides find many ways to communicate!

Setting Up a Guides Meditation Circle

I personally have found it to be incredibly effective to do spiritual work in a group setting. There's just something about it. The vibes go higher and an infectious, supportive energy is cultivated that helps everyone in the room to grow together.

If you'd like to try this, see if there's a group in your area that you could join. If not, you could create one of your own, even if you don't feel qualified to do so. It needn't be complicated – it can just be a group of like-minded friends who gather together as equals. You can meet monthly in your homes, a spare room, a garage or a local hall.

When you come together, set up the chairs in a circle, whack on some meditation music and then either take turns leading a 15–20-minute meditation and prayer for connection or maybe have one person leading it every time. You could also set aside some quiet time for you all to meditate at your own pace. You could practise using your angel cards (*see page 154*) on each other and share feedback too. You could meet for two hours or so. It's the perfect way to grow and to create a community.

When you feel ready, you could create another group for your clients, students or even your family, where you lead the meditation and prayer, but it's best to get some practice in first so that your light warrior path becomes more authentic and aligned with integrity.

Warrior Workout

~ Take time to set up your connection with your guides.

~ To develop the connection, paint your guides or find an image you can use to relate to them. Place it on your altar, if you have one, or somewhere you see regularly.

~ Note down any guidance you've received from them.

~ Hoop together your like-minded friends and family and meditate.

Chapter 5
THE ARMOUR OF LIGHT

*'Everything in the future will improve if you
are making a spiritual effort now.'*
Paramahansa Yogananda

I'm here as your ally. I'm here to help set some things straight for you and share my experience so that you can be the light warrior you were born to be. What I'm about to share with you is essential knowledge in order to progress on the path of light.

I'm grateful to have come from a psychic background because it has given me invaluable tools that I haven't been able to find in other spiritual practices and pathways. I was lucky enough to be exposed to the Spiritualist Church in my teens, and soon after attending my first ever Spiritualist meeting, I was able to find a development circle – a group for mediums to develop their skills. I went there weekly and it was there that I learned to create and carve my connection with spirit. Many different ideas were shared, but we were also encouraged to find our own way of working. I went to a Spiritualist church on a weekly basis, too, and was able to see mediums from all over the UK come and demonstrate their talents.

One of the things I learned very early on in my journey was the fact that we (that's you and I) are the keepers of our mind and of our body. We get to choose what goes on in this incredible vessel that carries our soul and we are completely in control of our energy field.

I'll never forget one night when one of my circle-mates was overwhelmed by a particular form of energy. I remember it like it was yesterday because it was such a profound lesson for everyone who was there.

Shaz had been coming to the circle as long as I had, which was about eight months at the time. She was a single mum – a super-fun and cool one. She always wore awesome outfits and had natural creativity. She also had a real interest in all things spiritual.

That night, just after we'd shared feedback on what we'd received in meditation, our teacher guided us to open our senses to the spirit world and all of a sudden Shaz became distressed. We all forgot about what we were doing and looked at her, trying to figure out what was going on.

'There's an energy over my shoulder,' she said, 'and I don't like it. It feels like a man. He's getting too close and...'

At that point she went to get up, as if to run away. She was sitting right next to me, and if you want the truth, it gave me the willies.

Our teacher said, 'Take control of your energy and your situation, Shaz! Don't let anything take your power away!'

Shaz heard her, but she was struggling. She was beginning to get really frightened and it was overwhelming her. It reached the point where she couldn't even listen – our teacher had to stand up and walk over to her, put her hands on her shoulders and reassure her that everything was okay. Then the feeling faded, and what a huge relief it was for us all.

That night, internally I vowed never to throw anyone in the deep end of spiritual practice without them being sufficiently prepared. We must learn how to deal with energy first, and that is what we're going to do here.

Because of stories and movies about 'ghosts', most people are scared of delving into the spiritual realm. They're afraid that they're going to be haunted or possessed or have a spirit attach itself to them.

You might think that was what was happening to Shaz, but there wasn't a bad spirit hanging over her or taking over her energy, she was just being exposed to energy and interpreting that energy in a fear-based way. What she didn't realize at the time was that she was fully in control of the experience. Like me, she came from the *Buffy the Vampire Slayer* generation. We saw demons, ghouls and weird entities on TV every week, which absolutely influenced our expectations of spiritual development. (Might I add, Buffy is my hero!)

The point is that when dealing with energy on a spiritual level, it's up to us to set the precedents. We have much more control over our experiences than we might think.

You Are the Keeper of Your Energy

Over the years I've been appalled by the irresponsibility of mediums and psychics in the mainstream media. I've witnessed mediums on television being 'taken over' by spirits in the name of entertainment, when the truth is that what's happening to these mediums is either good acting, psychosomatic response or, if it's really happening (which I highly doubt), it's purely based on their will. Do you honestly think if a spirit had the opportunity to come back through with a message, they'd want to scare a bunch of people who are recording a TV show with night-vision cameras? I don't think so either.

As spiritual practitioners, we have not only to honour and respect ourselves, but also all of those who have worked so hard to get psychic development where it is today. Less than 75 years ago in the United Kingdom, mediums were being tried under the Witchcraft Act and jailed as 'spies' because of their incredible psychic ability. We have to honour our spiritual heritage and everything our ancestors fought for, and I'm sure you'll agree that entertainment was not *their* intention – illumination was.

There is a purpose to our connection with spirit, and it's to help us evolve.

What has frustrated me is that many lightworkers have shied away from developing their psychic awareness because some mediums and psychics are making a mockery of what can be an extremely powerful and healing connection that can be beneficial to so many in this world.

I'm sharing this here not because I'm in judgement mode,

but because I want to lay to rest a fear that doesn't need to exist. I believe that developing intuition and psychic awareness is important for the light warrior journey because it's with these skills that we can hone in on our guidance, work more deeply with our angels and guides and also deal effectively with energy of a lower vibration.

When I teach spiritual development I make it clear – and it's important that you really own this from the word 'go' – that *you* are the keeper of your body and your energy body. It doesn't matter what energy is out there, good or challenging, it cannot – and I repeat *cannot* – enter your field unless you give it permission.

You need to know this now to remove any fear-based roadblocks that will stop you from progressing spiritually.

You also need to know that when any type of energy gets too much, you have every right to declare that you are in charge of what you feel and you can take control back into your own hands.

For some reason, most people take a passive approach to spiritual development. They seem to think that angels, spirits or whatever energy we are working with is in charge. I'm not sure where this has come from, but the truth is that we are allowed to have a say in what goes on. For me, being a light warrior is about becoming active in pursuit of the highest good.

In order for us to be the light warrior we feel drawn to being, we have to learn to care for ourselves and know that we don't have to be weighed down by everything we feel. We are entitled to ask for less energy, or more energy, and that's it.

Knowing we have this ability can take away many fears, concerns and reservations we may have about experiencing energy.

Just last week, there was an example of this when I was in Germany, working with a small group on connecting with angels through ceremony and prayer. During the two-day event many of the group felt as if they were in a space where they could let go of a lot of old emotions and it was such a joy to see them release them.

We also allowed selected people to work on bringing through love, messages and guidance from the angels. One of the ladies I invited to do this was Anna. She had been interested in spiritual work for over a decade and had done everything from shamanic work to swimming with dolphins. She was an amazingly dedicated spiritual practitioner and at the same time highly sensitive.

As she stood in the centre of the circle, I asked everyone to breathe deeply (I taught them Ujjayi), close their eyes and allow their palms to open upwards so that they could not only hold energy for Anna, but also share it with her. I then asked her to close her eyes and guided her through my routine of receiving messages from the angels. It's a simple technique based upon tantric invocation.

I said, 'Feel the angels drawing close to you now – visualize it. Imagine that an angel is standing so close to you that eventually they become one with you. Let their love in. And as you feel their love entering your energy, open your eyes and look for the person in the circle you are most drawn to work with.'

Anna found a lady called Lora.

'If you were an angel and could see through their eyes and look lovingly at Lora right now, what would you want her to know?' I asked.

All of a sudden, Anna began to fill up with the most incredible love. The whole group felt it. It was beautiful, but it was also overwhelming for Anna. She began to cry and couldn't get her words out. This became an important lesson for them all.

'Anna,' I said, 'place your hands on your heart. Reclaim your body as your own. Say mentally and out loud that you feel this energy, you feel this love, and it doesn't have to be this intense.'

Anna followed my instructions and very quickly the intensity began to die down. Her voice was back and she came thundering through with a powerful, evidential and enlightening message for Lora from her angel.

She told her that her angel was there to boost her confidence and to help her step back into her voice. She said it felt as if she had had her voice taken away from her and for many years it had been as if she had faded into the background. (That was why she herself had felt that she couldn't speak for a moment.) She told her that this wasn't why she was here and that she was a wonderfully loving person who had made a difference and was continuing to make a difference. It was time for her to reclaim her voice.

During the message Lora sobbed as she released all the pent-up frustrations and energy that were standing between her and her highest good and her voice of truth.

When Anna had finished giving the message, I encouraged her to thank the angel for their love and invite them to step back. She did so and said she could feel that the energy had gone.

In my eyes, the love Anna felt for Lora that day was an angelic love – a higher love, a love that the human mind and body can't fully comprehend. It's a love that is so powerful that our system goes into overdrive when we feel it. What I've come to learn is that unless we are clear and tell the angels, guides or whatever energy we're working with that it's too much, they will never know.

I like to think of our energy system as a remote control for the television. We have many channels, we have a volume button and even an off switch. We need to learn how to use this so that we can remain full of energy and do the work we feel called to do.

So, whenever a certain energy gets too much for you, even if it's energy from an angel, take control. Just tell them that you can feel them and that it doesn't need to be that intense. Alternatively, if you feel the opposite – that it's not loud or clear enough – you can ask for more. (*Check out Chapter 9 for more on this.*)

Psychic Protection 101

As you progress along the path of the warrior, it's important that you learn how to protect your vibes and ensure that you are working from the space of love. You need *psychic protection*.

When I first heard about psychic protection, I thought about the TV show *Charmed*, where people fought against dark entities and demons, but psychic protection isn't about that at all, it's about creating a positive atmosphere around yourself so that you can align yourself with the highest vibration possible and safely face your fears, knowing that you have support with you at all times.

Psychic Protection vs Dropping the Shields

There's a difference between shielding yourself and protecting yourself, and it's important to have this straight before you endeavour to man your spiritual artillery. Once you get that clear, you can really enhance your spiritual connection.

The shields I was speaking about earlier are the thoughts and thought processes that come from a fearful place, a place where you think you can be hurt. For example, you're going to meet a difficult family member and you know that it could be a volatile situation, so you prepare yourself to be hurt, i.e. based on a feeling of fear, you put up your shields. But, as you now know, shields are basically sticky webs of energy that attract more drama, fear and hurt to them.

Psychic protection, on the other hand, is about claiming your space and remembering your wholeness. It's about welcoming divine energy into your energy field so that you ultimately don't take on any unwanted energy from people you love, people you work with, environments you're exposed to or even worldly disasters that you've read about in the paper or seen on the news.

With psychic protection, you just declare that you aren't taking on the heaviness of a situation so that you can work with your own incredible light. When you do this, you clear any fear-based shields you have and create new ones that are formed purely from divine love. So, guess what they will attract?

Weird Vibes Are Not Your Responsibility

From this you can see that with psychic protection, what you are protecting yourself from isn't usually some dark force, but energy that may drain you or leave you with unnecessary baggage.

Here are a few examples. Have you ever walked into a workplace and felt intense anxiety come over you? Or walked into a room and known that someone there isn't in a good mood? Or gone to a hotel for the weekend with a loved one and got the feeling that something strange once happened there? Or had a conversation and walked away feeling the other person had sucked the soul right out of you?

That's what you want to protect yourself from – weird vibes that are not your responsibility. Weird vibes that stop you from fulfilling your purpose. Even weird vibes that you can help with, but don't have to be affected by.

**You can choose not
to take on weird vibes.**

Working as a professional psychic for many years, I gained a lot of experience in dealing with weird vibes! During my hour-long angel readings I would see traumatic events and uncover deeply emotional experiences. If I'd taken on every single emotion or energetic bond in those sessions, I'd have been drained beyond belief.

As a light warrior, your role is to face your own fears and ultimately lead those around you to the light. You must do this in a way that honours your being and your energy, and psychic protection is a way to do it safely.

Learning How to Protect Yourself

Although you have angels and guides who will keep you safe on request, keeping yourself safe on a psychic level is down to you. In accordance with the law of free will, your angels and guides cannot energetically protect you unless you ask them or explain, usually through prayer, that you are in need of help.

Many people get frustrated with this and say, 'They aren't called "guardian angels" for nothing.' But you must realize that guardian angels can't do everything for you, because this is *your* experience. You have to make your own decisions. Make sure that one of them is to keep yourself safe through psychic protection.

Here are some of the most essential and up-to-date psychic protection techniques I use on my own warrior pathway. They are more powerful than my previous techniques and I now share them with my clients and students the world over.

Clingwrap Theory

When I first started studying spiritual development I learned that before conducting any spiritual work I would need to invoke an energy of protection to keep my own energy safe, especially if I was working with people who were facing challenges. I would do this by visualizing myself in a bubble of light. I also did it in my daily life.

However, I was often putting on psychic protection, but ending up drained anyway. It puzzled me. It even made me upset, frustrated and annoyed! I decided to drop into meditation and ask spirit for the answer.

I was told loud and clear that most of the time I was asking for protection far too late and was 'clingwrapping' the draining energy in my energy field. Yes, I was locking it in, just as you might put clingfilm/plastic wrap round a sandwich to keep it fresh...

Talking of lunch, imagine you've met a long-time colleague for a bite to eat and during the meal they spill the beans on how challenging their life is. During the conversation you find yourself getting drained by the 'negative' energy. What's happening is that it's attaching itself to you. So you invoke an energy of protection. But then you're protecting yourself *and* the energy connected to you and locking it in.

**When you put on your protection too late,
you could be locking in the bad juju!**

So what do you do?

⟫⟶ Cleanse, Tone, Moisturize ⟵⟪

Here's a three-step psychic protection process that actually works. It will create an armour of light around you.

I based this process on a daily skincare routine. You know the one – the cleanser gets rid of all the muck and grime, the toner firms up the skin and the moisturizer locks in all of the goodness. You can do exactly the same with your energy.

Cleanse

First you need to cleanse your energy of any leftover vibes that aren't serving you – anything that's hooked on or attached to you from a challenging conversation, place or person. There are a couple of ways of doing it:

- You can imagine sacred fire energy coming from Mother Earth and burning away any unwanted energy that is attached to you. As it touches the fear-based energy, it transforms it from fear to love.

- You can ask Archangel Michael and/or the angels to cut the cords of energy that are holding you back or are attached to your energy field by saying a prayer:

   Thank you, Archangel Michael and angels, for cutting the cords that bind me to people, places, energy, situations and any other stuff I no longer need. It feels so good to know you are here. I am safe and free!

Tone

Toning is all about firming up the goodness that is already there. When it comes to toning your energy, it's about focusing on an aspect of your present positivity, or harnessing a blessing, or choosing to remember your current state of goodness. This ignites the warrior energy within.

Claim your wholeness by declaring that you are completely in control of your body because it's the vehicle of your soul. You can say this in your own words, but make sure you are speaking in the present tense and *really* putting your foot down. Let the universe and your guides bear witness to the incredible inner strength that you were born with.

My favourite declaration is powerful, simple and effective:

   I am the keeper of my mind and body.

   Wherever love is present, fear is a stranger.

   Love is here!

When I say, 'Love is here,' I tap my heart three times so I can feel a physical response to what I really know deep within me.

Moisturize

When you are moisturizing your energy, you are essentially putting on a coating that you know is going to lock in the goodness. This is the step that everyone knows from books and healing modality trainings, but it won't be as effective unless the previous steps have been taken. There are a few ways to do it:

- You can declare that there is an armour of the holiest light surrounding your whole body and being, extending 10–20 feet (three to six metres) in each direction.

- Imagine a cloak of light in the colour of your choice swirling all over your body or imagine yourself in a suit of shining armour from head to toe. Again, make sure that the protective light you create radiates out about 10–20 feet beyond your body in every direction. Really bring that into your vision and intention.

- Call on your guides and thank them for protecting you and the energy that surrounds you.

And that's the best way to keep your energy strong and clear!

Top Tip: Having said all this, I often still forget to do this process and find myself in situations that feel draining. What I do then is politely say, 'Can you please excuse me for a moment? I really need to go to the bathroom.' Off to the bathroom I go. I lock myself in a stall, do my three-step protection process and go back feeling safe and energized.

Saying 'No' is Spiritual Protection Too!

Saying 'no' is just so powerful! There's no doubt about it. Assertiveness is a quality of spirit.

Saying 'no' can be challenging, though, because when someone is asking you for something, sadly they have the expectation that you're going to say 'yes' and so it's very easy to feel obliged to do just that, even when you don't want to and know it isn't right for you.

But, especially as a light warrior, you need to make sure that you're speaking from a space of authenticity. Saying 'yes' when you mean 'no' can build up baggage and resentment, and this is essentially venom. It's a form of self-sabotage and can stop you progressing along the road of self-respect and self-love.

Truth is the language of spirit.

It's important to know that you're not responsible for everyone and everything. Owning this truth will allow you to act with integrity and honour your own self.

I believe when people approach us with a problem, it's a learning opportunity for us both. It could be an opportunity for us to be of service (if we really feel the call) or it could be an opportunity for us to stand our ground. For the other person it could be a lesson in asking for help (especially if it's not like them to) or it could be a lesson in standing on their own two feet and facing their own life lessons.

When I decided to start taking time for my growth rather than taking on everyone else's lessons, I felt more connected to my own angels and that my guidance was coming through more clearly than ever. I realized it was important for me to learn how to say 'no', but also to do it in a loving way. Here's how I do it:

If it's someone I love, I say:

I want you to know how much I love you and how much I care about you. I want nothing more than for you to be happy. But right now I can't help you with that. So I'm going to have to say 'no' to you, so I can say 'yes' to me.

Thank you for respecting my decision.

And then if they're there in person, I'll hug them. If they're on the phone, I'll say:

For the rest of today, I dedicate all of my prayers to you!

If it's someone I don't know, it's pretty similar. I'll say:

I'm sorry to hear you're going through a hard time and I will pray for your happiness and freedom. Right now I can't help you with this and so I am going to have to say 'no'.

Thank you for respecting my decision, as this will let me continue on my journey of self-care. I wish you well!

If I've said any of these to you, thanks for understanding. I'm sure you've been in my shoes. Remember that we're here to honour and be honoured. Make it happen.

Saying 'No' to Spirit

Many intuitive people, healers, psychics, mediums and lightworkers in general feel a duty to serve spirit. Hopefully one of those categories covers you. If so, first of all I want to honour you for that, because it takes courage to follow this calling.

With that being said, doing this work is not a *requirement*, it's a conscious *choice*. And so we have every right to say 'no'.

This was something I didn't realize early on in my spiritual development. I remember being overwhelmed in public places by the feeling that I had to deliver messages or healing to random strangers and wondering how I could initiate the conversation.

You may know the feeling yourself. In your daily life you may often see someone who needs your help. You might get an internal prompt that the person who is serving you in the supermarket needs a message or a healing session or who knows what. You know that you can help them – but you also know you've got a busy schedule. Nevertheless, for some reason you feel obliged, because daily you ask spirit, 'How can I be of service?' and here ya go – they're giving you an opportunity to serve.

The ego loves to make us do whatever we're asked by making us feel guilty if we don't. But that's ego. And we don't have to do what it wants.

We have free will. It's *spiritual law*. Spirit has to honour our decisions.

One day I just decided that enough was enough – and it all just stopped.

✕ *Prayer for Saying 'No' to Spirit*

> *Thank you, spirit, for understanding that I am unable to share this message today. Today I am choosing self-care.*

If you're feeling the call to be of service, shift your perceptions and turn your miracle mind on. Ask to be of service in a way *that will serve you.* (*For more on this, see Chapter 10.*)

Ultimately, your role as a light warrior is to see your own stuff, bring light to it and heal inside and out, and this is part of your service to the whole world.

Spirit needs us to be clear.

Psychic Attack

While we're on the subject of protection, I want to address this craziness, because it is given far too much time and attention than is needed.

First things first. I really believe in personal responsibility and the spiritual law of karma. These are two critical aspects to understanding what psychic attack is and if it's even possible.

Now I know for a fact that scientific studies have been conducted into the power of the mind and it's been proven that when we think lovingly about a family member (even if they're on the other side of the world), their brain will react as if they're receiving a real-life hug. With this being proven, think what can happen if we think the opposite. That is what psychic attack is. It's when someone is having consistent negative thoughts about you and you are experiencing it physically and/or emotionally.

Now this can happen, but I believe it can only be as powerful as we allow it to be. Most of my clients who have felt some sort of overwhelming negativity find it increasing when they find out about psychic attack – and it's not because the person involved is doing more of it or has become more powerful, it's because they really believe that someone has power over them.

If you think someone's psychically attacking you, the first thing to know is that it might not actually be conscious. They could really just dislike you or something about you (most probably through jealousy) and be using that to avoid thinking about their own problems. Therefore this is a call for compassion.

Now there's probably a part of your ego-self that wants to shame them right back or send all the bad vibes straight back to them. Truth be told, this experience is an opportunity for you to *claim your own power back* instead and learn how to become a serious black belt in psychic protection.

What about karma? Yep. We're going there. Here's the deal: there's more than likely a part of you saying, 'Well, karma's gonna get them for this,' and it may, but you worry about your karma and let other people worry about theirs.

Instead, consider the responsibility of both parties. I'm not saying you deserve what's happening to you, but you gotta learn how to protect your vibes!

You are in control of your vibes. You can tell trespassing energy to step back!

Also remember that even if the other party does know they are sending attack thoughts your way, or anyone's way for that matter, it's *never* going to make them feel good.

Invoking the Strongest Form of Love You Know

If ever you feel that you've been left vulnerable, exposed, wide open and have no idea what to do next, this is what you do: you invoke the strongest form of love you know.

This can be the love of your favourite saint, deity, ancestor, guide, loved one in heaven or loved one on Earth. And when I say 'invoke', I mean you draw them into your being or drum them up from within. When you draw pure unconditional love into your being, no fear can exist. No weird, stray, negative, scary or controlling vibes can rock you, because *love* is your core.

Whenever the stuff hits the fan, I draw on the strongest form of love I know, and for me it's Jesus. Although I don't call myself a Christian, I have a great love for Jesus. I feel that he was one of the greatest light warriors the world has ever seen. His entire existence was based upon love, forgiveness and service, and his energy is pure love. I feel that when I call upon him, his sacred love is so powerful that anything that's not love will be transformed by it.

Recently I was working with a client from the Middle East. When I was connecting with her energy, all of a sudden I could feel energy impressing itself on me that didn't feel good. It was heavy, dark and to many it would seem frightening.

I explained what was happening and she instantly said, 'You are psychic, you are real – you are picking up the family curse.'

I was completely thrown, because that's not something you hear every day.

It turned out my client had had threats from someone who was working with a 'black witch' to send negative energy to her whole family. Because she had come from a superstitious background, she believed that this energy could cause major damage to her life, and so did her family, which was falling apart. One of her children, a young adult, had stopped speaking to her, even though they lived in the same house, because of this 'curse'.

Clairvoyantly, the energy appeared black, which didn't seem good, but I knew that it was man-made and that my client and I could change it by invoking the strongest form of love we knew. So I told her about my love for Jesus. I told her that Christ energy was the ultimate energy and would transform any negative energy into divine love.

I also told her that this curse was only having an effect because she believed that it was possible and it was important for her to know that she was actually giving it power because she believed it was more powerful than she was.

I like to imagine Christ energy as a bright golden light. I told my client this and that we could imagine it consuming all of the fear, anger, frustration and any other negative energy connected with this situation.

I guided her to close her eyes and said a prayer, something along the lines of:

Thank you, Jesus, for drawing close now with your golden Christ energy and for bringing the miracle we need to change this situation.

Thank you for consuming all fear, anger and frustration with your most sacred love and transforming it back into divine love. We welcome your presence and your miracles now! Thank you.

And so it is!

Internally, I saw a golden light coming and taking all of the darkness away. My client began to sob, and when she regained her composure she said she'd seen a huge flash when I was saying the prayer and she'd known then that things had changed.

Later I was pleased to hear that her family relationships had healed and everyone was getting on again (apart from the normal hiccups that all families have) and that they had moved on from the idea that they were cursed. Invoking the love had healed the situation.

⟫⟶ Invoking the Love ⟵⟪

What's the strongest form of love you know? Maybe, like me, you love Jesus, so Christ energy is the strongest form of love you know. Maybe it's the love of a favourite saint or even a family member in heaven. Bring something in from your own experience – that's what makes this practice powerful and authentic.

- With that strongest form of love in mind, I encourage you to create a little prayer, in your own words, to that person or being. You can use my prayer above as an example if you wish.

- Imagine their energy circling around you. Feel the love.

Know that this love is the love you can call upon when you feel low, overwhelmed or lost – when you are in need of a miracle.

A Course in Miracles says, 'Everything that comes from love is a miracle.'

Make this a daily practice. It's beautiful, heart-warming and comforting all at once.

———————

Light Armour

When I'm putting on my psychic protection (cleanse, tone and moisturize!), instead of imagining a field of protection around me, I often imagine I'm wearing armour, as if I were a Samurai warrior, or one of the archangels. I see myself in an indestructible protective suit that will keep me safe in mind, body and spirit: *light armour*.

Choosing to put on light armour is an act of self-love. It's a conscious decision to wrap yourself up in light and keep any stray energy at bay. Make it a daily spiritual practice. The more you keep yourself safe and well, the more energy you preserve for the people that matter and for your purpose, which is ultimately to be happy. More on this later, but in the meantime, choose to put on your light armour and keep your vibes shiny and happy.

Another thing I do, if I'm needing extra protection, for instance if I'm in a building I know has a lot of potentially overwhelming energy, is to imagine swords of pure light, like the sword of Archangel Michael, swirling around me really quickly. My vision holds the idea that if any fear-based energy comes close, it will be cut away from my energy before it even tries to connect. That's powerful and effective for a fireball like me!

When I'm working with a group, if the ladies don't identify with wearing spiritual armour (as they often don't), I encourage them to imagine themselves as goddesses draped in the most incredible silks, with crystals of sparkling light that attracts only light-filled experiences.

What do you want to wear?

⫸⟶ Putting on Your Light Armour ⟵⫷

What about your light armour – what would you like it to look like? Why not take some time to meditate on creating it?

Is it like your favourite archangel's armour? Or that of an ascended master, goddess or god? (You could use my *Angel Prayers* oracle cards or *Keepers of the Light* oracle cards to help you with imagery.)

Do you have something circling the periphery of your energy, keeping everything behind it safe and strong?

Your armour is all about feeling safe and standing in your own light. Use your creativity and warrior essence to create something that feels right to you.

———

Warrior Workout

~ Get working on your Psychic Protection 101. Add it to your morning routine before you head off to work or do the school run. If you're working on an energetic or spiritual level already, add the three steps into your preparation.

~ Practise your three-step protection process in a safe place so that you are equipped when you are on the move.

~ Remember it's fine to say 'no' – even to spirit.

~ Practise invoking the strongest form of love you know.

~ Have fun creating your light armour!

Chapter 6
SHADOW WARRIOR

*'We can never obtain peace in the world if we forget
the inner world and don't make peace with ourselves.'*
THE DALAI LAMA

Warriorship isn't just about demonstrating external bravery, it's also about being honest with ourselves about our past and present so that we can grow beyond them. It's about having the courage to go inside and work on ourselves and face the stuff that we know we've been putting to the back of our mind, or even avoiding completely.

I personally believe that all of us on a spiritual path know what we need to work on, and to be honest, often the major reason many of us put it off is because when we finally deal with it, it allows us to enter an even more powerful state where we really can do the work. For some reason, we've been avoiding that as well.

Something I put off for a long time was addressing my weight issues. I was absolutely successful in avoiding them completely. When I was a teenager, my doctor told me I was obese, but I didn't do anything about it. Apart from using the excuse that I was more than a body and the only thing that mattered was my spirit!

When I look back, I was trying to push all my concerns about my body into the background, even though really I knew that this was just avoiding the truth. It took a while before I realized that the outer work I did on my body would reflect back and help my inner self as well. I could create a synergy of balance and love that would move through me mentally, spiritually and even physically. Duh – why did it take me so long?

I think that most spiritual people will agree that if we avoid something long enough, eventually our spirit will make sure we wake up to it, and often these experiences are traumatic. Who wants that? So, if we can do the work now – if we can enter a state of bravery now – it will help us avoid trouble and clear the obstacles that are blocking us from achieving our greatest potential.

The Shadow

This kind of work is shadow work. What is the shadow? It's an energetic space within that seems locked away. It is all the aspects of our personality and life that our ego doesn't want to admit to – anything from a deep dark secret to a traumatic memory, a deep wound or a talent that's not been recognized. It's the defensive voice that shows up whenever an 'unacceptable' aspect of our character is challenged or brought to the surface.

How the Shadow is Created

We create our shadow ourselves, from very early on in life, based upon what we consider good and bad, right and wrong.

As we create our self-image, who we think we are and who we think we're not, we reject certain aspects of ourselves as unacceptable and push them into the shadow. We make these decisions based upon what we believe to be true, regardless of whether it actually is true or not. In fact misperception is shadow's BFF.

For example, say you call yourself a 'spiritual person' and you have certain ideas (true or not) about what it really means to be spiritual, you will cast into your shadow all the aspects of yourself that don't seem to be spiritual to you. If you feel being spiritual means you can't say 'no', even if it causes you pain, then your capacity to be strong and truthful can be pushed into your shadow. (*If so, see page 192 for the remedy.*)

I know one person this happened to on an extreme level. They believed that being spiritual meant that they had to be still, accept everything and be calm at all times. But in reality they were the least calm person I knew (and that's not a judgement, it's an observation).

Every time they were exposed to anything that made them uncomfortable, instead of saying truthfully how they felt, they repressed their feelings because they were 'unspiritual'. Then they'd start to get stressed out, but still pretend to everyone that they were 'totally calm'. If anyone told them they seemed stressed, they'd even say, 'I'm not stressed, I feel very still and calm!' This voice was the shadow speaking.

So it went on and they got pulled deep into the shadow space, where they suffered greatly.

One day they came to me and asked for support because they felt that either the divine wasn't hearing them or they were 'too blocked' to hear divine guidance coming through.

What was happening was that the more they were repressing natural aspects of their personality in order to be 'spiritual', the further they were from being authentic. Connection to their true self had been lost, so it was no wonder they were struggling with the connection to the divine. They had lost all integrity.

Any need we repress or any part of our natural personality we reject will also become part of our shadow. We may insist we're fine, but if we continually avoid aspects of ourselves, it can eventually feel as though there's something missing. And there is: *authenticity*. We aren't our authentic selves.

It's not only unwanted traits that end up in the shadow space. Talents and gifts can also be there. For example, say you have an amazing talent for singing, but those around you mocked it when you were a child, or maybe you felt that it was an impractical gift and so you didn't develop it and just got on with your schoolwork instead. Later in life people may tell you that you're a wonderful singer, but you don't believe them or you brush it off, or the modesty of your ego says, 'Nah, that's not me.' This is shadow too.

When you begin to explore the shadow, you'll see things that are familiar, things you've forgotten about and things that are gifts. You'll uncover gifts that are sacred and special – gifts that will allow you to shine in the world.

**Shadow work can reveal strengths and
gifts you never knew you had.**

Light Attracts Light

To understand the workings of the shadow is also to understand the workings of energy. Everything in this world is comprised of energy, and that includes us. Every aspect of our being is energy – our spirit, our ego *and* our shadow.

As I mentioned earlier, like attracts like, so our energy draws towards it energy of a similar nature, according to the law of attraction. Our energy is constantly being shaped by what we think, feel, believe, know, speak and share, and is attracting energy accordingly. That's how our thoughts and feelings create our life. But what we repress is part of our energy too. Everything we reject – every wound, trauma and unforgiving thought – is also creating our life.

This is where positive thinking *does not work*. We can't positively think away our shadow – in fact, that's how it was created. Ignoring an aspect of ourselves or taking the traditional advice to 'just pretend it didn't happen' is essentially how we came to have a shadow in the first place.

This isn't a reason to feel guilty – it's human nature to repress parts of ourselves and we can use our *spiritual* nature to heal ourselves.

Activating the Shadow Warrior

'Repression' can be a scary-sounding word. For me, the shadow isn't negative, though. It's just fear that has been repressed and is camouflaging itself in self-defence. Its best chance for survival is the use of its favourite weapon – avoidance – and so the best medicine to heal this part of ourselves is essentially the truth. Once we shine the light of truth into the darkness of the shadow, we can reveal its treasures.

A light warrior doesn't fight darkness but shines light upon it.

It can be emotional to reveal what we've hidden away from ourselves and so there's a great chance that resistance will also show up like an old friend. But this work doesn't need to be as dark, scary and frightening as you might think. I believe shadow work, like all healing, can occur naturally. Walking our path with integrity will inevitably reveal aspects of our shadow to us so that we can release them. Honest, loving and revealing conversations and enquiry will do the same. Even when you're reading books like this, parts of your life you know you've disassociated yourself from will begin to come up in your mind. This is shadow work.

Cultivating a spiritual practice allows us to move into our shadow space in a safe way. Through meditation and self-reflection, we are able to delve into these hidden and repressed aspects of ourselves in order to heal and grow.

It's important to know that this work is not instantaneous – it's a lifelong process of self-love and self-enquiry – but it's absolutely doable.

What are Self-love and Self-enquiry?

I'm guessing you know what self-love is anyway, but I wanna share this with you as a reminder, because it's essentially the light warrior path.

Self-love is the daily spiritual practice of authentically appreciating ourselves and understanding our value. It's about allowing our vision of ourselves to go beyond our physical state into accepting that we are an incredible spiritual being filled with unlimited potential. It is essentially quietening the fear voice within (the ego) and accepting that we are already whole.

Self-enquiry is the process of asking ourselves important questions. It can be anything from tapping into our intuition when faced with a decision to sitting down and asking ourselves if a relationship is right for us. It can happen anywhere, but is wildly effective during meditation sessions and when entering ceremony. The only thing we need is the willingness to admit the whole truth and nothing but the truth!

The point is that when we want to step back into our truest power, we have to take ownership of our life and our energy system, past, present and future – we have to be willing to see it all.

The Light Has No Shadow

When I set out to create this book, I came across an awesome little picture quote online. It was a picture of a match being held close to a wall. The matchstick and hand holding it created a shadow on the wall, but the flame of the match had no shadow. The quote said: 'The light has no shadow.' *Booom*. I was prepared.

I already knew this book was going to be called *Light Warrior* and I knew I was going to speak about outshining the shadow. Now I had what felt like a wink from the divine!

Light does indeed have no shadow. It has no shadow on a physical level and none on an energetic level. Light is light. It's pure goodness.

Bringing Light to the Shadow

The coolest thing is that when shadow energy is exposed to light, it can become light, and once it has become light, it can't ever become shadow again. This is something I've clung on to and it's been so helpful along the way.

So, how do we expose our own shadow to light? How do we bring light to it?

Sometimes just seeing that we have something buried deep in our shadow is all we need to do. At other times, we have to be willing to embrace our shadow – to embrace everything we've rejected in order to make ourselves whole. This can bring up some fears and be a little uncomfortable, but it's important to know that the space being created is actually space for light to shine more brightly.

Be ready to see the light and shine on.

The best way to create space for shadow work is through meditation. Do this somewhere where it is safe for you to be yourself. You might want to do it alone or you might prefer to be with a partner. I recommend doing shadow work with a close friend or spiritual buddy who also needs to do this, or, if you have the resources, a wonderful coach or therapist.

Personally, I take shadow work into ceremony with me. In sacred space held by the elements and angels, I delve deep within in order to face aspects of my shadow energy and safely bring them to light.

More on setting up a ceremony later, but first it's important to learn ways of bringing shadow work into your daily practice.

✕ *Bringing Light Prayer*

Guardians of the four corners,

Mother in the Earth, Father in the Sky,

Angels, ancestors and warrior guides,

Thank you for bearing witness to this declaration of my spirit.

I choose to drop all shields of defence and let your light in.
Thank you for helping me illuminate anything I have hidden within the shadow,

Thank you for helping me reclaim lost gifts, strengths and aspects of my being.

Into my vision now, I allow all that I need to know to be revealed.

I am ready to see.

⟫⟶ Self-enquiry and Journaling ⟵⟪

Look at the questions below and take some time to figure out which feel relevant for you. You may want to move into meditation to consider them more deeply or to sit with your journal, relax, breathe deeply and ponder them for a while.

Through this process of self-enquiry, let your intention be to see anything that you need to see. There will be some surface stuff coming through anyway (especially if you have used the prayer). Know that this is an exciting process of discovering more about yourself and preparing to shine!

- Where in my life do I pretend to be content when I'm not?

- What conversations am I avoiding?

- What do I avoid remembering?

- What feedback are others giving me about my behaviour?

- What gifts are others seeing in me that I haven't recognized?

- What does my ego tell me I'm not?

- What memories do I pretend never happened?

- What strengths have I not been willing to see?

- What gifts have I held back from revealing or developing?

- What talents have I been embarrassed to share?

- What is it I really want to share with the world?

When stuff comes up and you see, hear or feel aspects of your hidden self being revealed, know that your spiritual sight is developing.

Write down what you need to work on and share what has been revealed with a close one, coach or spiritual teacher.

≫———→ **Invite in the Miracle** ←———≪

When you begin to face shadow energy, you have an incredible opportunity to create miracles. *A Course in Miracles* defines a miracle as 'a shift in perception'. It's essentially the moment you bring in light and see more clearly.

For me, shadow work is like peeling the layers off an onion. Bit by bit, you remove all of the stuff that stands between you and your freedom.

What then? You are left with a strange open feeling… The best way I can describe this is by comparing it to when you've just come out of the shower and wrapped yourself in a towel and there's someone at the door. You try to answer the door while standing behind it, but all of a sudden the wind pushes it open and your towel is about to fall off. You feel threatened, exposed, vulnerable. Any moment you could be naked in front of a stranger.

In shadow work, your ego is going to love that vulnerability, because it presents a moment for it to sabotage you, make you scared or, even worse, feel alone.

At that moment, declare:

I make way for miracles!

I use this affirmation whenever my ego likes to get loud and boisterous. I take back my power, invite in miracles and remember that *I* am the keeper of my mind and my body.

If you like, you can also call in the strongest form of love you know via a prayer (*see below*).

You are essentially changing the frequency of your energy, and therefore what you're attracting.

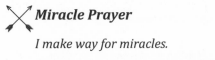 ### Miracle Prayer

I make way for miracles.

Where darkness once was, light now enters.

I call back my power, my presence and my love.

Wherever you are, wherever I have left you, I call you back.

If I have forgotten you or given you away, know that I cherish you now.

Into my heart right now [say this with feeling!] shall enter the strongest form of love I know. [Name this if you like.]

As the Earth is my witness and the universe my guide,

Today I move back to wholeness with the presence of angels holding me.

And so it is!

⋙⟶ Light Warrior Meditation ⟵⋘ with *Pran Mudra*

This is a light warrior meditation that I do often to bring vitality, energy and sheer goodness to my vibes. It can be done anytime, anywhere. I've done it in the middle of the park, on trains and even in airport lounges. I always feel energized afterwards, even if I only do it for two minutes.

Pran Mudra

Pran stands for *prana*, which means 'life-force'. *Mudra* means 'sign'. *Pran mudra* is 'life sign'.

Mudras are powerful yogic hand and finger positions. They can be practised sitting, standing, walking, lying down, in meditation and in yoga. They have been shared in many schools of yoga, including Hatha, Kundalini and Ashtanga.

You've probably done a *mudra* without even knowing it. Ever brought your hands together in prayer and bowed? Ever brought your thumb and forefinger together in meditation? If the answer is 'yes', then indeed you have.

Here's how to do this one:

- With both hands, bend both your pinky finger and ring finger in towards your palm and cover them with your thumb.

- Keep your middle finger and pointer finger extended and together.

According to yogic teachings, this activates the base chakra, which grounds and energizes you. It's as if you're plugging your system into the Earth and receiving a charge-up.

Pran Mudra and Ujjayi Breathing

Combining these two allows you to bring the energy of fire into your meditation. This warms you from the inside out. Wouldn't you like a zingy feeling that trickles through your vibes like you've just dropped three triple espressos?

You can do this sitting or standing. I like to sit.

Remember, you can record the steps first and then take yourself through them if you wish. It's super-simple, though.

Stage 1: Charge Up

With your hands in *Pran mudra* and your Ujjayi breathing on (*see page 21*), imagine that you're hooking yourself into the Earth below you. I like to imagine that there are roots going from me deep down into the heart of the Great Mother.

Do this for as long as you need. Two to five minutes is usually enough for me.

Stage 2: Blast Off

Once you've got the charge feeling, staying in *Pran mudra*, lift your arms upwards with your fingers pointing upwards.

Take a massive in-breath and then open your mouth to exhale all the *prana* around your energy.

The meditation is now complete.

Warrior Workout

~   Spend time learning more about the shadow. There are some wonderful resources online.

~   Do some shadow work by yourself.

~   Spend time working on your shadow with a friend, coach or therapist.

~   Bring the light warrior meditation into your daily practice

Chapter 7
FACING FEAR

*'I learned that courage is not the absence
of fear, but the triumph over it!'*
NELSON MANDELA

Fear is a funny old thing, isn't it? It's something we've all felt. I believe it reminds us that we're all equal. It gives us a space where we can be compassionate towards one another.

I've seen people break down the word 'fear' into False Evidence Appearing Real, whereas I've always broken it down to Forgive Everyone And Release. Either way, fear is very real in the sense that it's a feeling we all know, and yet in most spiritual teachings we're taught that it's *not* real. *A Course in Miracles* states, as I mentioned earlier, that only love is real.

I really do believe that our very essence is love. Fear is what happens when we don't remember who we are.

Fear is just a feeling, but it's a feeling that can make us lose our mind. It can make us feel alone and separate. It can make us feel that we have no control over events. That our instincts are shaky. That we are literally shaking! And it can appear in many shapes and forms...

Forms of Fear

Anxiety and Daymares

I struggled greatly with anxiety when I was younger, especially in my teenage years. I'd be walking down a street as it was beginning to get dark and nausea would sweep over me from head to toe. Then I'd start to get really uptight and wonder if a person on the other side of one of the doors was going to chase me or hunt me down. It got to the point where I couldn't go far without intense anxiety taking over. It was really debilitating.

Anxiety occurs when we have a desire to feel safe. We want to protect ourselves, but we can't control what's going on around us and don't know what might happen.

Daymares are anxiety's cousins. These are those moments of temporary insanity when we begin to think about our own worst nightmare or the worst possible outcome of a situation.

I believe both anxiety and daymares occur at times when we are incredibly sensitive due to an excess of negative energy in our energy field. This could have come from anything, even just high levels of stress. When it happens, I believe our own energy will do what it can to process it, perhaps by creating negative thought patterns or generating a feeling of concern in our belly. It might feel as though our insides are churning, but on an energetic level I believe our solar plexus (our fire centre) is creating fire and heat to burn away what it doesn't need, in this case negativity.

Even if you think you're a robust person and can deal with life's events, if you are experiencing anxiety or daymares, either you have deeper stuff going on internally that needs your attention or you have way too many negative vibes attached to you. (*Don't freak out, just hop back to page 66 for some Psychic Protection 101.*)

It's important to deal with anxiety and daymares on an energetic level, because if they become ingrained in your energy system, they'll begin to contribute towards your experience of life. Now don't worry if they already have – this can be undone.

When anxiety or daymares step up to me these days, I take the warrior approach, and I invite you to do the same. One of the ways I deal with them is to see them as fear and acknowledge them (*see page 108*) and the other way is to let the energy out, using the roaring breath (*page 41*) and the Mahakala–Kali *Kriya* (*page 189*) so that I can step into my warrior light.

Nightmares, Sleep Paralysis and Night Terrors

Let's talk now about these sensations, which are never good for anyone.

Nightmares are basically scary dreams – dreams that have scary things happening or are full of the feeling of being chased, or falling, or even dying. The images are produced in the mind and aren't real, though they can appear very real at the time.

Sleep paralysis, also known as night terrors, is another frightening feeling. It's the sensation that occurs when you wake up but you can't move or speak and you feel something is hovering over you that may cause you harm. Some say it's demons or bad spirits visiting you (but it certainly isn't). Some people have even described having a vision or hallucination where they think there's something watching them, and it can have an incredibly strong impact on their future time of rest.

Again, I believe all of these sensations occur because there's an excess of energy circulating in our energy field and in order to process it we go through a scary sensation or our fear hypes the energy up so it appears more powerful than it really is.

I really would like to get clear here that I don't believe any of these sensations are demons or ghosts or whatever the heck you want to call them. It's just energy expressing itself and people experiencing that energy in a state where they haven't taken full control.

Having said that, I know these sensations aren't pleasant. I experienced all of them when I was younger and I'm glad they (mostly) stopped by the time I was 16. (Sleeps paralysis is more common in young adults, because we're more sensitive to energy at this time.) I've had a few nightmares since – it happens to the best of us – and one night terror, but I'm honestly convinced that it was nothing sinister.

These experiences are definitely *not* down to evil demons having a go at us, but what they can be is our own demons coming up to be dealt with. Essentially, we externalize an internal fear that we're working through.

When this happens, especially if it happens on a regular basis, it's a major soul call for us to delve deep within, do some shadow work and face our fears. The techniques in this book offer some ways to start.

Feeling Haunted

When I was younger, I used to see spirits very clearly. At night I would often feel that there were people calling my name or wanting to speak to me. It created an 11-year fear of the dark.

I was very uptight about ghosts, because I used to think that spirits and ghosts were the same thing. Now I know they're totally different.

A spirit is the soul of someone. When a person's 'in spirit' that means they're back in connection with infinite love. When they go to spirit, they can watch over their loved ones on Earth, but haunting them will be the last thing on their mind.

Ghosts are people's old energy and memories playing out. They are actually just old vibes hanging around. So a ghost doesn't have to be a dead person – it could just be a person whose energy has made an impact on a place, or even on a person.

Here's an example: you go to a new location (though it's actually pretty old) and as soon as you arrive, a cool sensation comes over you and you say, 'This place is haunted.' It probably *is* haunted – but not by spirits or bogeymen, by old memories and energy.

That's not to say that these can't be pretty intense, sad or angry. And as energy beings we can be affected by these vibes, but if we're following warrior protocol and/or have followed our Psychic Protection 101, we can detach from them at will.

If we haven't done our Psychic Protection 101, it's never too late to follow the three-step process. In fact it's important, because if we don't, our sensitivity could lead to us becoming magnetic to old energy that wants to be healed or resolved, and that's when we'll feel as if we're being haunted.

I also believe experiences of 'being haunted' can be caused by our own over-excitement. We hype everything up and then scare ourselves.

I've been lucky enough to go on many 'ghosthunts' through writing a column for a newspaper. One evening I was sent with a bunch of 10 other journalists to Edinburgh. We were put up in an amazing five-star hotel that was actually an old mental institution. And because I was known for my psychic abilities, I was put in the attic that used to be the isolation ward.

Everyone knew but me. They wanted to see me get scared, but what scared them even more was me coming down the next morning to breakfast proclaiming I'd had the best night's sleep I'd had in years.

I believe I slept well because I knew how to look after my energy and avoid picking up any fear-based memories that could have been embedded in the energy of the old ward.

Not only that, I made sure I got my angel team to do a sweep of the space and make sure that all that wasn't love was brought back to a state of love. Thank you, angels!

I honestly think people's 'ghostly' experiences or other strange encounters are actually a manifestation of their own fear reaching what can be a dramatic climax. I believe if I had been afraid that something was going to haunt me in that attic, if there had been a possibility of it happening, that internal concern could have attracted it, or even created it.

Now I know that there are people who have never believed in ghosts and still had ghostly encounters. It does happen – but I believe that what happens is that they're exposed to a low form of energy or pick up a low energetic memory and their own energy processes it or tries to get rid of it, and that makes them feel as though there's an intruder in their energy field.

Ghostly energy isn't always negative, though. There can be positive 'ghosts', which are essentially loving memories that have been left in a space.

A client of mine contacted me recently to share an experience. He'd recently split with his girlfriend. The decision had been mutual and there was still a lot of love between them. One morning he'd been drifting in and out of sleep when he'd started to see what he could only describe as 'impressions' of his ex-girlfriend. He said it was as if her memories of her old routines, and even her smell, were filling the air.

We can leave long-lasting impressions on each other and also on our environment. Since we are the beings who create these impressions, we are also the beings who can perceive them. It's not super-sensory, it's normal. We just haven't realized that yet.

Spirit Visitation

But what if a spirit *is* actually visiting you? It's important we speak about this too. It is a possibility. But don't be scared. I remember my old teacher always used to say to me, 'It's the living you have to be frightened of, not the dead.' That's something I've always kept in the back of my mind just in case my ego goes for a wee run with my imagination.

What I've learned is that the spirit 'world' is a state – a state of being filled with absolute joy, happiness and contentment. When we move to spirit, all our earthly concerns, fear and sadness are left behind, because they can't exist in that state of love. So spirits want nothing more than for us to be happy and they would never do anything to scare, frighten or harm us.

I've also learned they must respect our free will. If a spiritual being makes themselves known to us, we have every right to ask them to step back and leave us alone. They won't be offended, because they can't be – they're in a state of absolute love.

It's a relief to know this, right?

You are the keeper of your body and mind – rock that!

Demons

I'm rolling my eyes because this is so ludicrous, but I have to cover this subject because it's important to clear up all the stuff you hear about it and also a lot of the questions that come up for the many people who have come to light work from a religious background.

People often say to me, 'If you believe in angels, you have to believe in demons, right?' And then the longwinded discussion begins...

Where to start? To help us understand the concept of demons, it's good just to refresh our idea of angels.

Angels are the thoughts of God. They are essentially love expressing itself. Within love, no fear can exist. The teachings of the Qabalah state that when we think of someone positively, we actually create an angel and send it to them. So angels are extensions of love.

Got that?

Demons are just the opposite. I don't believe they come from some lower entity or world – they are just expressions and extensions of fear and torment. Almost like a bad cell that's grown and grown, a 'demon' (and I really want to use this term loosely) is just some negative energy that's grown and grown. Every time someone comes across it and is scared of it, their fear feeds it and it becomes larger and larger.

Now here's how it gets interesting. This is also a reminder of how brilliant our mind is. In order for our human intelligence to get a handle on something that cannot be seen as a human, we give it an identity. So, when angelic energy comes along for example, in our mind we imagine it looking a certain way or having a certain type of personality, etc., etc., and we do exactly the same with an energy that feels of a much lower vibration. The senses feel it and the mind gives it an identity and then the hype is created and you have your horror story, but in reality it's *just energy*.

A woman tried to argue with me over this recently when I was visiting Norway. I'd been invited to give a talk on energy awareness and I included a section on busting some of the myths that surround fear, demons and dark stuff. Everyone in the audience was doing spiritual work and I wanted to give them some tools so they could guide their clients, should they have any challenging experiences similar to what we've just discussed.

When I explained that I believed our personal beliefs and fears could influence these experiences, a lady stood up in protest (it happens from time to time!) and told me that what I was saying was wrong because she had been possessed. She told me that a 'beast' had had to be removed from her. 'And if it hadn't,' she added, 'I wouldn't be here today.'

After a lengthy discussion, it turned out that she'd had a very strict Catholic upbringing which had left her with a fear of being possessed by a demon. In fact throughout her life she'd been told by her family that she was a 'little devil', and whenever she'd done something wrong, she'd always had the feeling that it wasn't her doing it, but 'the devil' taunting her. So wham bam, thank you, ma'am – she had that experience.

What I'm trying to get over here is that the mind is very powerful. That's *our* mind – *we* are ultimately in control.

We need to know that if we are to answer the call for light. Sometimes we outshine the darkness by figuring out what's causing it in the first place.

Dealing with Fear

Over the years I've found that spiritual practice gives me the opportunity to deal with fearful thoughts and sensations from an internal perspective, and I hope that should I ever need to deal with fear on a physical level, say if I'm involved in an accident, I'll be better prepared because of all the mental work I've done.

Even though I know I can never truly prepare for the unknown, one thing I do know is that even if my spiritual practice isn't able to change a situation or a fear or a loss, it will hold me through the healing. I know that it's the reason I'll recover, and I'll definitely recover better with it than without it.

I believe dealing with fear is also a wonderful contribution to mental health. I don't believe that fear is the primary cause of mental health concerns, but I do believe that tapping into the warrior within can really help our mental wellbeing.

Let dealing with fear be your warrior training. Let it be an opportunity to move into the love that created you – the love that you are. Let it be your chance to become the incredible warrior that you are.

Fear is an opportunity to stand up and stand strong.

On the subject of incredible warriors, I'm a big fan of the Buddha. I think he was a super-rad dude who was an answered prayer for many. He experienced fear just like you and I, and there's a story about him that has been a real help to me in dealing with my own fear.

One day the Buddha was meditating in a hillside cave. He was going deep.

Outside the cave, one of his devotees was keeping watch. Everything was fine until he saw a demon called Mara coming up the hill.

'Uh-oh,' he said.

He began to figure out how he could keep Mara from the Buddha. 'Maybe I'll tell him he's out for lunch,' he thought. 'Or he's away shopping.'

Soon he was so lost in his thoughts that he was surprised when he felt something breathing down on him. He looked up.

There was Mara in all of his demonic glory.

Now Mara, as you might imagine, wasn't exactly a handsome looker. He was a demon and his tongue was out, he had blue skin and to be honest he was quite frightening.

'C-c-c-can I help you?' the guard asked.

'I'm here to see the "Buddha",' Mara replied, rolling his eyes and making inverted commas with his hands.

'He's... erm...'

The guard didn't know what to say. Then he was interrupted

'Let him in,' came a strong voice from within the cave. It was the Buddha.

Mara entered the cave and stood before the Buddha, who was sitting in the lotus position.

'I see you, Mara. I see you,' he said.

He looked at Mara right in the eye. Right down the barrel. He wasn't scared. He acknowledged him. He conversed with him. He accepted him. He allowed him to be there and found comfort in his presence.

This story is a huge mutha-flippin' metaphor. Let me break it down for you:

- You are the cave.
- Mara is your fear.
- The guard is your ego.
- The Buddha is the voice of your soul.

When fear appears, even though it's a creation of the ego, the egoistic response is not to let it in. Your ego wants you to *feel* fear, but it definitely doesn't want you to *deal with* it. It just wants you to be contained. So the lil' guard within you says, 'Pretend you're not in,' or makes you ignore it by focusing on something else or getting busy. This essentially buries the fear deeper and deeper.

But your soul is constantly connected to love. So, when you allow your soul to speak, fear has to stop in its tracks.

I believe that love and fear are just energy vibrating at different levels. Fear can only exist when we believe there's a separation of energy. If we see it and acknowledge it, we allow it to rejoin love.

When fear appears, look at it right in the eye.

Tell it you see it.

When you see it for what it is, you allow it to return home.

Fear is a feeling, but it doesn't have to take over. Maybe that's happened in the past, but that was then and this is *now*. You are the keeper of your mind and body. You are a light warrior. You can decide to let love lead. Only you.

Fear is a feeling and that's all it needs to be.

When fear appears in my life, I view it as a reminder from my body, the human me, how much I care. Fear is appearing because I am concerned about loss, or not doing well, or even separation. But both science and spirituality teach me that I am one with all. When I move back into oneness, I let love be my leader. I let love in and I share it with all around me.

⟫⟶ Warrior Practice to Face Fear ⟵⟪

Here's a practice for when fear strikes loud:

- Close your eyes.

- Tune into your breath. Breathe deeply.

- Switch on your Ujjayi (*page 21*).

- Speak loudly and lovingly to your fear. Here are some words for you to use:

  Dear fear, thank you for being here and for reminding me how much I care. I see you for what you are. I see you. I choose now to return to love.

_____

Back to the Altar

I want to share a powerful spiritual practice with you that will help you when it comes to dealing with your fears.

There's a common misperception that we have here on Earth. We think we are 'down here' and the divine is 'up there'. It seems we've been trained to think like that. So when it comes to asking for divine help, we have the idea that God has to descend upon us.

Now the one thing that both science and spirituality have taught is that we're all one – we are absolutely one with the entirety of the universe. So that means that even though it feels as though we're separate from God, we're not. Everything has God within it. So I believe that a fear only continues to be a fear as long as we allow it to be separate (in our mind) from God.

Working this out was a game-changer for me. But even as someone who has a strong spiritual practice, I still get pulled into thinking, *God is watching*, rather than recognizing, *God is actually within this experience*.

To help with this, I created the following spiritual practice:

≫——→ Bringing It Back to the Altar ←——≪

Sometimes my mind starts to get a little bit ahead of itself and I begin to worry about what will happen, how it will happen, when and where, etc., etc. So I've created an image in my mind of an altar. It's always an amazingly spiritual altar, but sometimes it changes style or location. Some days it's a shamanic-style altar in a forest and at other times it's a high altar in a huge cathedral. Wherever and whatever it is, I imagine it is dressed beautifully with crystals, statues, candles and incense – basically, it's a grander version of the altars in my home and office.

Whenever my mind begins to run away with something, I command, usually internally but sometimes out loud, 'Come back to the altar,' and I imagine myself grabbing the whole situation and dropping it onto the sacred altar in my mind.

Try it yourself. It's a really powerful practice because it's a visual reminder that even though a situation may feel separate from God, separate from love, especially if there's a lot of fear around it, it's actually not separate at all. When we place it on the altar in our mind, we allow it to be one with love in our mind, and that's the kind of thinking that creates miracles.

Calling Back Our Power

We've spoken a little about this already, but it's a big deal. Our power is our essence – it's the part of us that gives us that spark of energy and drive to 'go for it'. Although it's always connected to us, we can give it away, even if we don't realize it. This can happen when someone or something is trying to get the better of us or we've allowed someone or something to have a hold over us in a way that's stopped us from going for a dream, vision or goal.

My mum often says, 'Don't give them your power,' when I've been harassed by someone online or I've started to get frustrated by the way someone is treating me or someone close to me in my daily life. What she means is: 'Don't channel your energy into someone or something that's not going to appreciate your time or honour it in the slightest.'

I believe that on a psychic level when we pour a lot of energy into a negative situation in our life, we actually *leak* our own energy into it, and that's why we're often left drained or anxious – our energy has literally drained away.

However, our soul has an incredible ability to heal itself. Even if, say, we gave away a lot of our power a decade ago to an ex-partner, when we call it back, it will come back.

You know people often say, 'I want the old me back,' when they've been through a tough time? What they're really saying is they want their power back, because 'the old them' was full of life and energy and power.

I was recently working with a client who was finding it difficult to sort out her career. Leigh was a talented journalist, but was also brilliant at alternative therapies and was known for her accurate angel card readings too.

During the session we discussed all of her different options and the possible reason why she wasn't fully committing to any of them.

I remember getting the feeling that it was something to do with her power, but I decided to ask the angels for insight too. I remember hearing the clear message that Leigh wasn't allowing herself to be 'seen' and I got a vision of her standing in an invisibility cloak, almost like Harry Potter.

I fed this all back to her and she said it made complete sense. She told me that she'd been brought up in an Evangelical Christian family who didn't fully agree with her spiritual ideas and choices. This had stopped her from being fully 'out there' and being seen for who she was in all of her power. She had felt called to a teacher/healer role, but had begun to do lots of other jobs on the side, including the journalism, to distract herself from stepping into that role and facing her family's judgement.

As I explained to her, she'd poured so much power into trying to win their approval of her sacred calling that she'd leaked it out and given it away. She'd become used to running on half-empty, and in order to be fully seen in the world, she needed to call her power back. I invited her to move into prayer with me to call it back for good.

It was an amazing experience. First of all it felt as though Leigh was cracking through a massive egg of uncertainty that was surrounding her. I felt it shatter and clairvoyantly I saw golden light zooming straight into her heart.

Leigh herself burst into tears as she felt herself receiving her own essence back and knew it was back for good.

Whenever there's a situation that's been bothering you and/ or you feel as though you can't pluck up the courage to tell someone how you feel, you need to call back your power.

When you choose to do that, you choose to top your energy up until it is overflowing. It's an incredible feeling.

✕ *Prayer to Call Your Power Back*

Dear power,

I call you back to the cave of my heart.

Wherever you are, wherever I have left you, I call you back.

Even though I may have given you away or had you taken from me, know that I allow you to return.

So it is that I am topped up until I am overflowing with my own light.

I am full of my own light, full of my own power.

Today I remember I have a choice and I choose to be happy in my own true light and power.

Thank you, universe and angels, for bearing witness to this reclamation and for supporting this process as I step back into my highest, greatest self, for good!

And so it is.

Warrior Workout

~ Work on your commands to let spirit know you're enjoying your own space.

~ Refresh yourself with Psychic Protection 101.

~ Take the warrior approach to fear.

~ Practise bringing situations back to the altar in your mind.

~ Call back your power – for good!

Chapter 8
WARRIOR CEREMONY

'I learned I could be both wild and holy.'
ANA T. FORREST

Ceremonies have been held all over the world for thousands of years. We love to use them to celebrate life, death and union, both romantically and spiritually.

They have also been performed to honour warriors, something that continues today in the military through the awarding of medals and ranks, while in tribal cultures, they have been conducted to keep warriors safe, connected and focused in battle and to guide them safely home afterwards, whether to their family on Earth or their ancestors back in the spiritual world.

As a light warrior, you can consciously choose to enter into ceremony – not to set yourself up for battle, but to create space for yourself to grow. Through ceremony you can tap into the wisdom that lies within, uncover some of your challenges and set loving intentions for your development.

Ceremony is like giving a megaphone to your prayers.

I've always had a fascination for spiritual ceremony and have involved myself in many facets of it. I've drummed with shamans and Druids, danced with white witches and howled at the moon. I've been initiated into Reiki, Kriya yoga and even Freemasonry. I've prostrated myself at temples in India, jumped barefoot over fires and immersed my body in holy water. I've been baptized into the Goddess at the White Springs in Glastonbury. Ceremony has been huge in my world and I want to take you there.

Sacred Space

Ceremony is about consciously creating a sacred space so that we can align body, mind and soul with the powerful forces that exist in the universe. In this space, we can set intentions, connect with our guides, do shadow work and open up to spiritual guidance. It can be in our home, office or somewhere in nature. One of the things I've found about sacred space is that it doesn't have to be large and fancy – in fact a yoga mat can be enough.

My yoga mat does feel like a special place to me. This 6ft by 4ft (1.2 × 1.8m) piece of rubber has a lot of magic on it. I've sweated on it everywhere from England to India. I've fallen on it, picked myself up on it and even turned my world upside down on it (by standing on my head).

Your sacred space can be anywhere from a magical place you visit to the lil' bit of space you have by the side of your bed. Even though it may not be physically very grand, the energy it can create can be incredible. It can become a vortex of sacred energy where you can align your frequency with the very highest.

Creating Sacred Space

Creating the right space is essential if your ceremony is to go well. I recommend a physically safe place where you know you won't be disturbed. You want to be sure you can stay aligned with your intentions, thoughts and spirit during the ceremony.

If you do get disturbed, don't think it's ruined the whole process, though. If you're performing a ceremony outside, you have to be willing to come and go with nature and the elements anyway.

To create sacred space, you have to clear the area of any old energy and any negative stuff that's floating around in the ether.

You have to clear the physical space too. If you're going to be working indoors, don't have anything lying around the space and ensure things aren't covered in dust. If the ceremony is taking place outside, make sure the space is cleared too. Correctly dispose of any litter and make sure you're not damaging the natural world around you.

Physical clutter equals psychic clutter.

Creating Ceremony

In order for you to step into ceremony, I feel it's important you recognize that your life is already filled with it. You perform small rituals every day.

I know that I'm a creature of habit and I follow regular rituals in my daily life. Every night at bedtime I go and flick the kettle on, then I go into my bedroom and take all the extra pillows off the bed and leave them on the floor. When the kettle has boiled, I make a cup of peppermint tea and I enjoy it in bed to bring myself down. Then I put some lavender and palo santo oil on my wrists, neck and chest (and sometimes my third eye) and I wind down reading a book. I say my prayers, do my Psychic Protection 101 and then prepare for slumber. This ritual brings me great joy.

We all have rituals in our life. How we get ready to go out, the routine of our week, the days we work out, or eat certain foods, or do certain hobbies, or see certain people… Life is filled with ritual. Even nature follows a ritual cycle. The sun rises and sets every day, the moon goes through a monthly cycle and the seasons move through the same sequence every year.

When you step into ceremony, you are aligning yourself with the movement of the cosmos. You are allowing your human self to connect with the universe.

And the real magic is you.

First Principles

There are some important principles to bear in mind if you want to have success with ceremony:

Have fun

Fun and happiness are the highest vibes you'll ever have. The more you enjoy your ceremony, the more you'll benefit from it.

Breathe deeply

The instinctive action to breathe will keep you aligned with your psychic and spiritual instincts. The deeper your connection to yourself, the deeper your connection to spirit.

Know that intention is everything

Ceremony is all about intention. Don't get worried or weirded out by what tools you have or don't have or what you're making your intentions with – remember, the real magic is you.

This is a spiritual practice – treat it with respect

Ceremony is fun and enjoyable, but to keep this energy aligned it's important to enter into it in a state of respect. Don't do it if you're under the influence of alcohol or drugs or are in a state of mind that's not working for you. If you're not feeling it today, best to wait until you're feeling more aligned with yourself.

You can't get the ceremony wrong – it's just about celebration

Here's the truth: ceremony isn't about following someone else's suggestions, dialogue or script. If you do, there's a chance you might fumble your words or forget what you were going to say. Follow your heart and you'll not get it wrong.

Entering Ceremony

The ceremonial practices I'm going to share with you here are an eclectic mix of different ideas and teachings I've learned along the way. I've strung together Celtic influences, Native American ideas and personal practices to offer you something that feels both sacred and authentic. I believe that warrior ceremony is all about finding what's right for you, what works for you energetically and what supports your intentions. At the end of the chapter there's an example to guide you, but it's really all up to you.

If you do energy work, you can bring ceremony in at the beginning of anything you're doing. Maybe you're giving someone healing, reading angel cards or even doing any of the exercises in this book. Whatever it is, creating a ceremony around it will allow you to have a deeper experience.

When I host workshops, I often begin the day with a smudging ceremony and an invocation of the elements, archangels and animal guides. I also welcome these into my yoga and meditation practices, often with incredible feelings of connection, so I'm including information on them here (*see below*).

The Four Directions and Elements

In ceremony we align ourselves completely with the energy that created us, the energy that moves through us and the energy that we have within us. Part of that involves attuning ourselves to the elements and everything that they stand for

In both Celtic magical practices and Native American shamanism, the honouring of the directions and elements is a common thread. Although the two traditions have different elements corresponding to different directions, the one thing that makes them similar is the fact that they are about respecting the cycles of nature. For me, being Celtic in origin and living in Scotland, it feels only right to follow the Celtic system, but my heart is drawn to Native American shamanism, as the first peoples of America really know the land like no one else. So I've found a way to bring both together.

In the Native American practices, they welcome the sun in the East, because that's the direction it rises in the world over. However, in the Celtic tradition, East is the element of Air (rather than the Fire of the sun), so I decided to stick with the Celtic tradition but at the end welcome the sun and moon (to bring balance) separately, to benefit from their support too.

So, here are the four directions and their correspondences:

North

North is all about the element of Earth and it's the space we can go to for grounding and support. Earth represents our physical body, our worldly possessions and our sense of belonging on the planet.

East

East has the element of Air and it's the space we can reach out to in order to breathe, 'clear the air' and collect our thoughts. Air represents our thoughts, our breath and our connection to the life-force that moves through us.

South

South has the element of Fire and it's the space that helps us ignite our will, connect with our passions and essentially 'fire up'. Fire represents the spark of life within us, our spirit and our ability to fulfil our desires.

West

West's element is Water, representing our emotional self, our intuition and the blood that runs through our veins. Water allows us to connect with the wisdom of the body and the intuition of the soul and express our truest self in the world.

⤬ *Welcoming the Elements Prayer and Chant*

Welcoming the elements and their energy into a ceremony doesn't have to be wildly dramatic or complex. It can be done with a simple prayer, something like:

I welcome the Earth energy in the North, the Air in the East, Fire in the South and Water in the West.

I am grateful to be held in ceremony by the elements of life.

There's an old pagan chant that's so simple I often sing it when attuning to elemental energy. You may hear other versions of it, but the one I use goes like this:

Air, my breath; Fire, my spirit,

Earth, my body; Water, my blood.

You just sing and sing and sing until you are completely entranced by the energy the repetitiveness of this song creates.

Archangelic Gatekeepers

Another cool thing to know about ceremony is that you can use it to connect with angels. When you create sacred space and welcome the elements into it, you can also welcome archangels in to stand in the cardinal directions. This creates incredible energy, like a force-field, in which you can enter deep meditative states with the archangels holding you.

The archangels I welcome into the four directions are the four major archangels that everyone knows and loves.

Archangel Uriel

Direction: North
Element: Earth

Although Uriel has been known as the angel of the sun, he holds the energy of Earth rather than Fire. He has the capacity to help us connect with our own body in a way that feels inspiring and exciting. He is a strong archangel who will help us feel physically revitalized and strong.

Archangel Raphael

Direction: East
Element: Air

Raphael, the angel of healing, governs the intuitive connection and the awakening of the third eye. His presence can help us align our thoughts, intentions and intuition so that we feel alert and clearly connected on a mental level to spirit and our guides.

Archangel Michael

Direction: South
Element: Fire

Michael is the angel of protection, but also the angel of Fire. He can help us direct our will and fulfil our heart's desires. His presence can help us burn away any concerns, fears or challenges that stand between us and our growth. He will make us feel warm on the inside and focused on the outside.

Archangel Gabriel

Direction: West

Element: Water

Gabriel is the mother of the archangels and her presence makes us feel safe, as if we are in our mother's womb (which is filled with fluid). She helps us delve deep into our emotions so that we can truly listen to our feelings and understand how we can express them in a loving way in the world. She helps us connect with our inner child, so that we can express ourselves without our ego holding us back.

Animal Protectors

If archangels are the guardians of the spirit realm, animal totems are the protectors of the nature realm. What I've learned this far on my journey is that not only should we be connected with spirit for guidance, but also with the Earth and its messengers. So I encourage you to welcome your animal guides into ceremony too.

I've picked eight Celtic animal guides that I call into ceremony with me and I'll share them with you here:

North (Earth)

Stag – a guide who brings strength, perseverance and drive.

Snake – a symbol of transformation (the shedding of old skin) and the capacity to adapt to an environment.

East (Air)

Hare – has a connection to other worlds and psychic intuition. The hare is famous for being hypnotized by the moon (moonstruck), hence its connection to all things psychic.

Raven – allows us to gain insight and understand symbols, signs and secrets.

South (Fire)

Fox – always has a plan (although sometimes a cunning one), so can help us address our needs and fulfil our desires.

Wolf – is all about teamwork, moving as a pack, or having to fulfil a mission alone. The wolf is resourceful, uninhibited and wild. With wolf energy, we can be in full view or camouflaged in nature.

West (Water)

Salmon – a symbol of spiritual courage and strength. The salmon swims upriver using nothing but will against the current, so can help us get to the places within that seem difficult to reach.

Swan – the beauty, grace and poise of swan energy can help us move into a space of complete and utter acceptance so we can reveal our internal beauty in a very external world.

The Sun and Moon

Drawing in the energy of the sun and moon can really help us connect with the energy of the cosmos.

The Sun

The sun represents divine masculine energy. With sun energy we can encourage our intentions to grow, bring things to life and warm anything that seems cold. Sun energy helps us tap into vitality, health, wealth and all things abundant.

The Moon

The moon represents divine feminine energy. With moon energy we can delve into our emotional and intuitive side. With the awareness we gain, we will be able to answer the call for light.

Smudging Ceremony

Smudging is an easy, simple and approachable ceremony that you can start with to build your confidence. It's a Native American tradition, but I was taught it by my Reiki master back when I was a teenager and it's something that's remained part of my practice ever since.

Smudging means lighting a sacred plant or herb and using the smoke it creates to clear a person's energy or the energy of a space. The herb represents the element of Earth, the lighter or match represents Fire, the smoke represents Air and the dish used to catch any ash and extinguish the herb represents Water. So this easy and accessible ceremonial practice allows us to connect with every single element in one process, and the smoke serves as a physical expression of what we are intending to change and create.

It's possible to smudge a person, an object or an entire home. My mother loves smudging with me and is often asking me to dust off her energy with the sacred smoke. She really feels the benefit.

For the best results, you should use a feather to help you direct the smoke, but you can also use your hand or a pocket fan. I recommend investing in a smudging fan if you feel you want to continue this practice. You'll be able to find an ethically sourced one online, or if you know any local shamans, ask them for one.

I feel the best plants to use for smudging are white sage or palo santo:

- White sage – A plant that is native to high desert ecosystems and grows strongly in California. For hundreds of years it has been widely accepted that white sage is a powerful purifier of lower and negative energy. This is medicine that has been shared with us by the Native Americans.

- Palo santo – This magical and mystical tree grows in South America. It has been used by shamans and wisdom-keepers to cleanse and heal both those who use it and those who are surrounded by its smoke. It's my favourite and less messy/smoky than sage.

As ceremony is all about intention, it's important to know the source of your smudging herb. There's no point using white sage or palo santo that's not fair trade – it just violates your integrity. With the internet, we have the capacity to search for fair trade stock so that we can really be in alignment with our highest intentions.

Also have some sort of fireproof dish in which to catch any stray ash and extinguish the flame. At home I use a large abalone shell and in my office I have a small brass cauldron.

It's important to make sure there are no smoke alarms or sprinkler systems where you intend to smudge, because you don't want to try to explain to a firefighter or your neighbours that you were 'clearing the space' – you will quite literally have done that if an alarm has been set off!

»——→ Smudging ←——«

This is how I smudge – based on Native American tradition, but in my very own style:

- Place whatever plant you are using into the dish that you will use to catch the ash.

- Hold it with both hands.

- Close your eyes and start Ujjayi breathing (*page 21*). (Remember to breathe throughout the ceremony, as it's easy to hold the breath in concentration.)

- Call on your warrior guides internally and thank them for guiding you in this experience.

- Set the intention that you are creating energy that will clear away any negative debris and facilitate healing.

- Light the smudging plant and give it a moment to burn, then blow it out.

- Use your fan or hand to waft the smoke over the person or space you're smudging.

- As you smudge, visualize yourself energetically clearing away everything that no longer needs to be there.

- When the smudging is complete, thank your guides and thank nature for her medicine.

———————

⟫⟶ Create a Smudge/Aura Spray ⟵⟪

There are going to be times when it's not ideal for you to burn plants or create sacred smoke to smudge with. That's when aura sprays become the best secret warrior weapon in your bag. You can pick them up in spiritual and health stores readymade, but I like to create my own. I often make them for events and leave them at the front of the room for the audience to use. I also whip them out in taxis, on aircraft and everywhere in between – they are so handy to have.

It's important that you make a blend that both feels right for you and smells nice to you. I recommend using organic alcohol to make one that will last a while. However, if this doesn't work for you, spring water and essential oil blends will last about five days before going off.

- To create a base for your essential oils, I recommend mixing 40 per cent organic vodka or gin and 60 per cent spring water in a jug.

- Once you've got your base, you can drop your favourite essential oil into the mix. I often use rose oil, but you can use anything really. My favourite right now is palo santo monk oil (you'll be able to find that online).

- Then pour the mix into a glass spray bottle (again you can find these online or in your local health store). I use 50ml bottles so I can take them on flights.

- Holding the mix in your hand, say a simple prayer, for example:

  Thank you, universe, warrior guides and Mother Earth, for blessing this spray with your tender loving care and for programming it to cleanse, strengthen and protect all the auras that it kisses. And so it is.

Then your smudge/aura spray is ready to light up some auras. Whack it in your bag and bring out whenever you need to clear any weird juju from the space around you or a friend is having a bad day.

Raising Energy, Raising Frequency

Once you've created sacred space and invited in the elements and archangels and your animal protectors, it's important to raise up the vibes. Old-school white witches called this 'the cone of power'. I love that idea. In ancient times, this was when drumming, dancing, singing and chanting would begin.

I can't tell you how to raise your personal vibes, but I'll list some suggestions for you. You'll discover your own way and that's absolutely perfect.

Yoga

If you are a yogi/yogini, this is a perfect time for you to practise. It's the moment when your sacred space becomes a 'sweat lodge'! Do a practice that's easy on the body but brings deep breathing, connection and a sense of expansion.

Music

You can bring your iPod or other music player into the space with you. Flick on your favourite high-frequency music (I love 'Spectrum' by Florence + the Machine) and dance in your magical space.

Another great option would be to play an instrument if you've got that talent and it makes you feel good. (Don't do it if you don't love it!)

Singing and Chanting

If you've got the voice, you may as well use it. Singing and chanting are actually the ultimate way to tap into vibration, because that's what the voice is – pure vibration. Chant or sing your favourite song, and do it directly from the heart.

Tap into Source

Ceremony is fun and it's a wonderful experience creating the space, but it's an even better experience soaking up the goodness you've created in this little vortex of energy.

Once you've raised up the vibes, you have the opportunity to delve into spiritual practice. Move into meditation, or a practice of connection, or whatever else you're working on. The space and energy you've created are sacred and now spirit will use this frequency to reveal all that you need to know. Use your guidance tools and check in with your intuition/internal teacher/warrior to receive information and guidance that will support your journey.

I recommend bringing in your journal and writing down anything that comes through, because often when you leave the space, you forget what you received. The reason for this is because of the high-octane frequency you've tapped into – it offers clarity in a way that you may not experience in your day-to-day life *unless* ceremony becomes a daily practice.

Now I'm not saying you have to perform a ceremony every time you do a spiritual practice, but commit some time to ceremony at least once a month and reap the benefits it offers you.

Aligning Your Ceremony with the Natural World

Choosing to align your ceremony with the seasons and the moon can be particularly powerful.

New Moon

Beginnings, setting new intentions

Performing ceremony at the new moon will allow you to tap into the cosmic energy of change. This is when the moon represents maiden energy – she is young, vibrant and full of life. As she moves out of darkness and prepares to grow over the two weeks, you can work with this energy to plant seeds of change in your life, set intentions for the months ahead and begin new projects.

Full Moon

Psychic awareness, healing and connection

When the moon is full, she is at her most powerful. She represents mother energy. The full moon allows us to connect deeply with our intuition and psychic awareness, and also with healing energy. When preparing to receive healing or much-needed guidance from spirit, you'll find it will always be best for you to do ceremony around this time, because your spiritual senses will be most receptive to this energy.

Waning Moon

Letting go, shadow work and release

When the moon begins to wane and move into darkness, she reaches the wise woman/crone stage. This is a perfect time to release old patterns, do shadow work and move beyond fears that may once have held you back. This is a quieter time energetically and will allow you to move deeper within and uncover anything that needs to come up and out for you so you can step into your wisest self.

Seasons

- Spring is all about preparing for the year ahead.

- Summer is all about enjoyment and vitality.

- Autumn is all about harvest and abundance.

- Winter is all about nurturing, retreating and replenishing.

Within this framework, you'll be able to find your own way to perform ceremony. This is what will make your light warrior practice real and authentic.

Being a light warrior is all about following your truth.

Closing Down the Space

I would say that learning to close down the ceremony and sacred space is the most important part of all. It can be easy to build it all up and do the practice, but you also have to honour the sacred energies that hosted the space for you.

Giving thanks to nature, the universe and all of your supporters on the other side is so vital. Not because they want to hear it from you or to be worshipped, but because gratitude is what is ultimately going to take you forward on your spiritual pathway.

For me, gratitude is the ultimate spiritual practice. Give thanks for your blessings – the blessings around you and the support you receive. I like to remember the term 'humble warrior' when I am in spiritual practice, and when I am in life, the humbleness will provide connectedness, and ultimately that's what will support you in your light warriorship.

Closing down the ceremony doesn't have to be a massive ritual – it's all about the intention. I finish every ceremony with a thank-you prayer – it just gives me the opportunity to direct the energy and give thanks to my guides in heaven.

⟫⟶ Light Warrior Ceremony ⟵⟪

Here's a light warrior ceremony that you are welcome to use, either as it is or as a template to create your own ritual.

When I perform a ceremony, I don't follow a script anymore, I just go for it, but this has taken many years of practice. There's nothing wrong with having a sheet of paper or a note to hand.

Using a compass (they're on most smartphones), figure out where the cardinal directions are. Then you can start.

Smudging

First of all, clear the space with smudging. You can look back to page 130 for more information on this, but I'll repeat the instructions here for you:

- Place whatever plant you are using into the dish that you will use to catch the ash.

- Hold it with both hands.

- Close your eyes and start Ujjayi breathing (*page 21*). (Remember to breathe throughout the ceremony, as it's easy to hold the breath in concentration.)

- Call on your warrior guides internally and thank them for guiding you in this experience.

- Set the internal intention that you are creating energy that will clear away any negative debris and facilitate healing.

- Light the smudging plant and give it a moment to burn, then blow it out.

- Use your fan or hand to waft the smoke over the person or space you're smudging.

- As you smudge, visualize yourself energetically clearing away everything that no longer needs to be there.

- When the smudging is complete, thank your guides and thank nature for her medicine.

Call in the Elements, Archangels and Animal Guides

Facing East:

(If others are participating, have everyone face East with you.)

Close your eyes. Imagine the power of the wind. Feel it rushing through you.

> *Guardians of the East, element of Air, Archangel Raphael, the hare and the raven,*
>
> *Thank you for your presence and protection. Your energy is welcome here today as I/we step into ceremony. Like a breath of fresh air, your light fills my/our lungs and I/we*

know that it will guide me/us towards deeper insight and understanding.

Raphael, great healer, you are welcome here. Thank you for being the guardian of the East and for witnessing this growth today!

Aho to the guardians of the East!

(*Everyone else can say, 'Aho!' which is Lakota for 'hello/thank you'.*)

Facing South:
(*Everyone facing South now.*)

Close your eyes. Imagine the power of fire and feel your passions burning!

Guardians of the South, element of Fire, Archangel Michael, the fox and the wolf,

Thank you for your inspiration and light. Your energy is welcome here today as I/we step into ceremony. Like a log fire, your light brings me/us warmth and inspiration so that I/we) can follow my/our desires and achieve my/our aims.

Michael, great protector, you are welcome here. Thank you for being the guardian of the South and for witnessing this growth today!

Aho to the guardians of the South!

Facing West:
(*Everyone facing West.*)

Close your eyes. Imagine the power of the great seas and feel your emotions!

Guardians of the West, element of Water, Archangel Gabriel, the swan and the salmon,

Thank you for your comfort and care. Your energy is welcome here today as I/we step into ceremony. Like the power of roaring seas, your light guides me/us to a deeper emotional connection, so I/we can express myself/ourselves clearly in the world.

Gabriel, mothering angel, you are welcome here. Thank you for being the guardian of the West and for witnessing this growth today!

Aho *to the guardians of the West!*

Facing North:

(Everyone facing North, yah.)

Close your eyes. Feel your body cementing down into the Earth. Feel rooted.

Guardians of the North, element of Earth, Archangel Uriel, the stag and the snake,

Thank you for your strength and grounding. Your energy is welcome here today as I/we step into ceremony. Like the Earth can shake, your light shakes out any old energy that is stopping me/us from reaching stability and clarity.

Uriel, angel of light, you are welcome here. Thank you for being the guardian of the North and for witnessing this growth today!

Aho *to the guardians of the North!*

Welcome the Sun and Moon

Welcome these luminaries with a prayer:

Roaring sun, shining moon, Father–Mother God

Thank you for bestowing your blessings upon this ceremony today and for witnessing any growth herein. You are welcomed with much gratitude and joy!

Raise the Energy

Now your ceremony is set up, it's time to raise the energy! You may want to do some drumming, singing, dancing or maybe your whole yoga practice. Do what feels good to you. Let the vibes rise super-high.

Perform Your Practices

Maybe the purpose of this ceremony is to practise yoga or maybe you'd like to carry out an exercise given in this book. Maybe you're creating ceremonial space to do an angel card reading or healing for a friend, or client, or even for yourself. Once you've raised the energy, whatever you plan to do, you're good to go.

Close Down the Space with Gratitude

Once you've finished your ceremony, give thanks to those who've helped you in a way that feels right for you. For me, one big closing prayer feels sufficient, along with a bow to each direction to thank all the guardians.

Standing in the centre of your sacred space, say the following prayer or something similar:

Thank you Father–Mother God, elements, guardians and anyone else who has helped.

I/we set the intention that whatever energy is left over in this space is taken to somewhere in the four corners of this world where it is truly needed. Today, I/we especially think of the children and animals of this planet that do not have a voice. May this energy allow their voice to be heard and may it provide a light that will lovingly lead them forward.

Thank you, elemental energies, for your synergy and support and for all the guidance that was received today. May whatever was received here today be to the benefit of all sentient beings through time and space.

I say all of this with the highest intentions and for the highest good.

And so it is!

Then declare:

This ceremony is now complete. Aho!

Warrior Workout

~ Take time to understand the basics of ceremony.

~ Spend time working out which intentions or practices you would like to enhance through ceremony.

~ Find time to acquaint yourself with your animal protectors or find ones you are drawn to.

~ Source materials so you can practise smudging yourself or your loved ones.

~   Create your own aura spray.

~   Figure out what will raise energy for you in an authentic way.

~   Step into ceremony.

Chapter 9
INTUITIVE WARRIOR

*'The intuitive mind is a sacred gift and
the rational mind is a faithful servant.
We have created a society that honours
the servant and has forgotten the gift.'*
ALBERT EINSTEIN

The intuition is the voice of the soul. I believe that it isn't a 'still small voice within', it's actually quite loud. Generally, though, we're not willing to listen to it or even recognize it. Nevertheless, I believe that whenever we have an issue or a challenge, our intuition is ready and willing to lead us to where we need to be, based upon the intentions we have set, either consciously or unconsciously.

The deeper we dive into spiritual work, the louder the intuition gets. The more shadow we shed light on, the more fear we face and the more willing we are to move into our light warrior self, the more prominent the intuitive voice will become in our life and the more we will benefit from its guidance.

As a warrior, you are encouraged to follow your intuition. Tapping into it will allow you to develop an even stronger relationship with your guides and angels. They will use it to share their message with you.

Developing Intuition

I believe that developing intuition is the same as developing psychic skills. I honestly believe being intuitive and being psychic are actually the same thing. Intuition has just become an easier way of expressing it, because the word 'psychic' can often trigger the idea of a fortune-teller sitting ready to tell your future.

Over the years of psychic development in my own life, I've come to see that the more time I give to my intuition, the more my intuition will give back to me.

Developing my intuition has generally been more down to commitment and discipline than anything else. That might not sound like fun, but I've made it entertaining by thinking of my intuition as a more enlightened version of myself – a sassier version, a voice of spiritual reason that can put me in my place if necessary.

Over the years I've worked with many techniques to connect with my intuition and although they're always developing and changing, one of my favourites is to meditate and go on an inner journey to the cave of my own heart. Inside the cave I imagine a bench, and on the bench, waiting for me, is the highest form of myself. He's sitting there, smiling, in bliss, ready to share with me what I need to know.

I'll often go on that little journey and sit on the bench and have a conversation with the highest form of myself, and I'll emerge with so much insight, guidance and support. It's really powerful stuff. I know the highest form of us has no form, but if creating an image to focus on is something that resonates with you, then I highly encourage you to try it for yourself. I've outlined it for you later in this chapter (*see page 156*).

But first, a little more about intuition itself.

Why Do We Need Intuition?

Have you ever had a strong sense of being pulled somewhere? For example, have you ever taken a different route than usual and found out later it was for a higher purpose or that by doing so you had avoided a disaster? Have you ever felt drawn to a particular section in a bookstore, only to find a new book that has had a life-changing effect?

Our intuition will direct us to where we need to be.

Our intuition works in mysterious ways and it will do everything it can to let us hear its guidance. It can not only push us, it can also prompt us to halt and hang back. Usually this is to help us avoid something that isn't what we intended or part of our plan here on Earth.

I was recently in the United States with my friend Meggan Watterson and one morning we were planning on driving from the Berkshires, in Massachusetts, to Maine to visit some friends.

We were just about to leave when I got a hit of intuition to check my wallet for my driving licence. And then boom, *I remembered I'd given it to a barman the night before to hold the tab open for our party. I realized that I couldn't leave it behind – it was essential I had it, as I was going to be driving in a foreign country.*

I looked the bar up online and called, but it wasn't opening for another five hours.

We had to set off on our journey, as it was going to take four to five hours to get to Maine, so we decided to head down to the bar on the off-chance. Honestly, it was as if my intuition was leading the whole thing.

The bar was indeed closed, but something prompted me to go round the back and there was a kitchen worker there who was able to help me recover my licence.

Then something in my head said, 'Just grab some lunch,' so I suggested it to Meggan. She's not as much of an eater as me, but she was happy to have a salad while I had something more substantial.

After that, we finally set off. On the road we were having so much fun listening to the radio and following the sat nav that it took a while before we realized there had been a huge crash up ahead only an hour earlier. If we'd left when we'd planned, we could have been right in the centre of it all. It was as if our angels and intuition were working overtime to keep us safe on our journey.

Sadly, we didn't make it to Maine that day. We'd wanted to see our friends, but to be honest we were both so beat from the week-long retreat we'd just led together that what we really needed was to chill. The universe knew that and the universe provided. We ended up going back to Meggan's for five days of relaxation in the summer sun.

Intuition, Prediction and Intention

Have you ever said, 'I knew that was going to happen!'? In fact you don't even need to answer me. I know you've said it, and probably quite a lot. I have too.

Here's how I feel it all works. Our intuition is in some way predicting our future, and it can do this because we have a hand in creating that future. The world we see and experience is based on our 'point of attraction' – what we're attracting into our life, whether we're consciously aware of it or not. The teachings of Abraham-Hicks call it 'the Vortex', and I really love this idea, because it gives us a clear vision of how it all works. Think of it like this – you have an energy surrounding you right now, and every one of your thoughts, feelings, intentions and beliefs is creating that energy, and it's completely magnetic and is drawing experiences your way, based upon what you're giving off.

So, when a psychic is connecting with someone's energy and is able to accurately predict events in their life, it's because that person's energy, or 'vortex', is creating those events. When I'm giving someone guidance and can feel their life going a particular way, it's based upon what they have in their energy system at that time.

To take a trivial example, say I'm working with a coaching client intuitively and I pick up a connection to a motorhome and they say that this is accurate, I may go on to say, 'I can feel that you're going to be in a motorhome or you'll be buying a motorhome in the next six months or so,' and they'll nod in agreement. The reason they're in agreement is because they've set an intention (or someone close to them has) to get a motorhome and I'm picking up on that intention. If it doesn't falter, they will have the motorhome.

The intention may falter of course. I recently saw Michael Bernard Beckwith speaking about something similar to this on *SuperSoul Sunday*. He was talking about how we can set an intention to have something, but unless we 'become' it, we'll probably lose it again. He used the example of people who win the lottery and then lose everything again. They set the intention to have money, but they can't allow themselves to become one with it, so they lose it all.

This lack of clear intention will have an effect on our intuition too. Our intuition gives us guidance based upon our highest good and the intentions we have. If we keep changing direction, it begins to get confused and can't guide us so well.

To make the most of this incredible inner guidance system, we need to state where we want to go. So, work out who you are and what you're intending to do, because ultimately this is what the universe is responding to.

The universe isn't giving you a plan, it's waiting for yours.

Dealing with Roadblocks

Not that it's always easy to follow your guidance. You know what it's like when you get a full-body hit that you're to go somewhere and do something, but on your way you get a load of setbacks? For example, you're going to a conference somewhere, but your car breaks down or you miss your flight or you get off the train at the wrong stop. We've all had this, right?

You might doubt your intuition and wonder whether the universe is saying, 'It's not meant to be.' It's in moments like this that I urge you to check back in with your inner guidance system. I'll often say something like 'Intuition, based on my intentions, is this still the right way for me to go?' and I'll usually get a feeling to either continue or stop.

If you get the hit to continue and there seem to be roadblocks ahead, what then? I believe the blocks are being created by ego, shadow and fear. They are actually hurdles that you have the opportunity to leap over. They are little opportunities to become stronger in some way. Life is asking, 'Are you sure you want to be this powerful?' Go for it!

Be clear and precise with your intentions and regularly root out any negative thought patterns or limiting language you're saying over and over, because that is what you are putting in the sat nav of your soul and that's where it will take you.

> *I recently worked with a client who had just been working for a company away from home. The deal had been that if she could make improvements in the overseas office, in one year she could return and take on her boss's job.*
>
> *During her time away she put her heart and soul into the job, met the targets, got the team working in harmony and altogether excelled at her job. But the whole time she kept saying to herself, 'I've not done enough' or 'I'm not worthy.'*
>
> *When it came to the end of her placement, she was so disappointed to hear from her boss that he couldn't give her the promised promotion that she came to me for advice.*
>
> *'I kinda knew that was going to happen,' she admitted.*
>
> *I replied, 'Of course you did.'*

I see this in my own life too. A thought pattern that I use all the time is *I'm going to be late*. Every day I seem to get myself all shook up trying to get to the office, the gym or even yoga on time. Even if I'm not running late, I keep affirming, 'I'm going to be late,' and the next thing I know, I am late. I made it happen.

If you ask for it, the universe will bring it to you.

I know this pattern is holding me back and I have to change it. So when I catch myself doing it, I think of my prayer of surrendering my day to the angels, which I say every day, and remind myself, 'Everything is happening according to divine timing.' Here's that prayer, in case you would like to try it for yourself:

✕ *Prayer to Surrender Your Day*

Thank you, angels and warrior guides, for surrounding me with your presence. It feels so good to know you are here.

I surrender my day to you, knowing that only good is happening now and coming!

And so it is!

If you have old thought patterns hanging around, old intentions that are obstacles on your light warrior path, you can also use this prayer:

✕ *Prayer to Clear Old Intentions*

Dear universe,

I am ready to release all of the intentions that have been standing between me and my highest purpose, which is to be happy.

> *Thank you for clearing my energy of these intentions now,*
> *as I align with what is best for me and live a life of love.*
>
> *And so it is!*

You can count on your intuition, but let it count on you too. Always be as clear and positive in your intentions as you can.

Inner Dialogue

The key to working with the intuitive voice in my opinion is creating dialogue with it. To do that, you have to make a clear distinction between the voice of intuition (love) and the voice of fear.

It's not always easy to make that distinction at first, but I've come to see that intuition is never in a rush and always trusts in divine timing. It will speak lovingly but also in a way that is strong, courageous and powerful. It does not waver, it's direct and to the point, and although it's a loving voice, it will crack the whip if it needs to, especially in a fight or flight moment.

The voice of ego (fear) is always in a rush. It has a time limit for everything, because it believes in limits. It will speak in a way that is like a warning and will promise failure 'if you don't do this'.

If you can commit to daily meditation, your intuition will come through more strongly than ever. Just taking the time to show up every day *for yourself* is the best gift you can ever give yourself. The more often you turn up, the more often your intuition will have the chance to download into you all that you need to know.

It's easy – you just have to start. Even if you think you're not good at meditation (which is a really unfortunate thought pattern, so clear it now), just begin. The rest will come from the practice. Your intuitive voice will eventually get quite loud, but you have to give it time. So begin now. Set aside five to 10 minutes every day just to turn up and say, 'Over to you, intuition!' and see what comes through.

Angel Cards and Oracles

Angel cards and oracles are a great way to develop your intuition and awareness. I swear by my angel cards. I was first introduced to them when I was just 14 and I got my first set for my 15th birthday. These cards have ultimately led me to where I am today and I'm just so grateful that I came across them.

Angel cards and oracle cards are basically a set of usually around 40-plus cards that all have an angel, guide or powerful message (or all three) on them. To work with them, you simply set your intention to receive guidance and then pick a number of cards to reveal a message.

I believe the cards will reveal to us what we already know, because our intuition has probably spoken to us about it already, but often we need a more tangible message, something that we can actually see, before we are ready to follow the guidance.

When I first got my angel cards, I would pick cards for *everything*, no matter how small, and this really helped me create a powerful relationship with them that has now been able to give both me and those I work with startlingly accurate messages.

As we get into the routine of picking cards regularly, we begin to pick cards we *knew* were going to come out, and that's because our intuition also develops a relationship with the deck and will begin to use its imagery, messages and keywords to unlock messages deep within us.

I believe that not only do we pick the cards, the cards pick us, based upon the spiritual law of attraction. Like attracts like, so when we're picking cards we attract the cards that best reflect our situation, strengths, gifts and whatever else is going on in our life.

This is good for working with the ego and the shadow too, because often we'll pick cards we don't want or cards we don't want to relate to, but there's always a message for us there and sometimes we need to stop avoiding things and become aware of them.

If you're working on developing your intuition and intuitive voice, I highly recommend adding an oracle card practice to your daily spiritual practice so that you get into the habit of asking for what you need to know. There are so many wonderful decks out there.

To boost what you get from your cards or oracle of choice, take them into a ceremonial space with you, choose to work with them on the highest vibration possible and approach them with integrity.

I'm lucky enough to have created my own oracle cards and I use them every day. Over the years, what I've found is the cards I pick are never wrong, but when I take the time to meditate and pray first, I find myself in a better space to listen to what they're offering up to me.

➤➤➤ Checking In with Intuition ⬅⬅⬅ and Your Oracle Cards

If you don't have an oracle deck, go and get some and come back to this section. I believe they'll become a powerful addition to your warrior practice.

Prayer and Intention

Keeping your deck and journal handy, first of all set your intention with a prayer:

> *Thank you, universe, angels, guides and anyone else who can help, for assisting me in uncovering any unheard messages from my intuition at this time.*
>
> *I am willing to see, hear and feel what I need to know in order to further my journey along the light warrior path. I welcome you to this space now.*
>
> *And so it is.*

Meditation

Now it's time to move into meditation. Close your eyes and just let whatever happens happen. Breathe deeply with the intention of being open and receptive to divine guidance.

- Imagine that you are going into a beautiful crystal cave. The cave is on a beach and sunlight is shining through the crystals and creating rainbows of light all around you.

- In the centre of this warm, well-lit, welcoming cave is a bench, and on the bench is the highest form of you. This is the real you, the spirit you, the you that is not separate from love and the you that can guide you with love.

- Sit down with them and ask them what you need to know. Take some time to hear or see anything they want to share with you.

- Once you feel as though you've had enough, even if you haven't heard anything directly, thank them for the experience and find yourself coming back to the here and now.

Once you've come back, take some time to write down in your journal what you experienced and any messages you felt were coming through.

Reading the Cards: A Three-Card Reading

- When you're ready, shuffle your cards.

- Place the whole deck on your heart for a moment. Imagine your love reaching into the cards.

- Then spread them out and pick three cards:

  The first card represents your strengths, your gifts and what you've worked on already. Know that this is divine guidance thanking you for committing to whatever this card is about.

  The second card represents what's going on in your heart right now – it's what your heart wants you to know and what will keep you focused on your intentions. Let what this card shows anchor you to the energy of love within you.

  The third card represents what you need to do (your challenge card). It's basically the thing you're avoiding or haven't recognized yet that will ultimately lead you to where you need to be.

- Take time to review each card, what's on it, what it's saying to you and what you *feel* it represents. It may be useful to take some notes as you work through them all.

- Once you've taken everything in, take a moment to close your eyes and thank divine guidance in all the forms in which it has come to you today. Commit to working on whatever your challenge card shows and invite your guides to help you.

The Warrior Stone Oracle

When I was learning to work with oracle cards, I also had a set of eight stones with little symbols on them that you could 'cast' like dice to create a little reading. They were called 'witchstones' and were often really loved by the people I did readings for.

When I started writing this book, I got the hit that I could develop a little warrior stone oracle that I could work with for guidance and inspiration. I had an idea that symbols would be involved, but I wasn't sure what I would use, so I went off to bed to relax and seek inspiration from other worlds.

I decided to put one of my cherished medicine bags under my pillow to see if its energy would encourage a dream journey that would inspire me. It is made of deer leather (sustainable and cruelty-free, of course) and has a little elk tribal design on it. Inside I keep two of my favourite crystals (a tanzanite and a small piece of golden spodumene) and a piece of palo santo wood.

That night I had a powerful dream in which I met a Native American shaman and watched him performing a ceremony. In front of us was a blanket that had a drum, an arrow and a broken arrow on it. In the distance I could see mountains and a great eagle was flying above us. Both the sun and the moon were high in the sky. I remember the shaman dancing as a snake hissed around us and a stag watched from afar.

The dream felt like an initiation of sorts. It felt inspired and guided. I felt that the different elements of it revealed the symbols for my warrior oracle and so I set off to make it.

Before work I headed to a local crystal store and bought nine flat agate stones (often called palm stones), then went to the craft store across the street and picked up some metallic marker pens.

After dinner that night I sat on the floor at my coffee table, created nine symbols and put them on the palm stones so that I had warrior guidance at my fingertips. What's weird is that I knew already what each of the symbols meant. It was as if the information was downloaded into me.

Here are the symbols and what they mean.

Sun

In many traditions the sun represents masculine energy – Father Sky – and joy, success, happiness and vitality in all areas of life. The Sun stone brings the energy of growth, of life, of newness. It is a strong and clear 'Yes!' that you are on the right path.

Moon

The moon represents feminine energy, intuition, insight, inspiration and the emotions. The Moon stone brings the message that your feelings are important right now. If any intuitive feelings are coming up, they are guided and correct. Follow them.

Mountains

Mountains offer the energy of stability and strength – they are unshakable and immovable, connected to the Earth and reaching up to heaven. The Mountains stone indicates spiritual strength, stability and the capacity to move beyond any challenges that have come your way.

Drum

The drum is the sacred instrument that allows shamans to journey between worlds. They use it to focus their intentions and delve deep into other realms. The Drum stone indicates deep inner journeys and the rewards of spiritual practice. When it appears, know that your journey is guided and that you're making great progress.

Arrow

The Arrow stone brings the energy of protection and intention. With its sharp edge, the Arrow allows you to disconnect from any unwanted energy and remain safe in moments of distress.

It also brings a reminder to stay focused on the highest intentions possible, because loving, positive thoughts will lead you safely to where you want to be.

Broken Arrow

The Broken Arrow brings the energy of peace – it shows there's no longer any need for defence against something that may have been bothering you for a while. When it arrives, it tells you that the energy of resolution is available – there's a perfect opportunity for a fresh start and an end to all negative dramas that may have happened.

Eagle

Eagles fly so high that they literally see things from a higher perspective. The eagle is also one of the most revered spirit guides in Native American teachings and for that reason represents spiritual growth and a message from our spirit guides or from the angels. When the Eagle stone comes your way, you are being asked to see your current situation from a higher perspective and invited to align your energy with the highest, because there is a powerful opportunity for growth heading towards you.

Snake

Traditionally, the snake is a bringer of change and also power. So when the Snake stone appears, you are being given an opportunity to overcome a dark aspect of your life, perhaps a fear, a shadow aspect or something that your ego continues to haunt you with. The Snake brings the energy of shedding, inviting you to face your fear and see it for what it is so that you can remove that old layer of energy from your being. This is a powerful symbol of transformation, but you are the one who will make it happen.

Stag

Stags have the capacity to survive in various terrains and move through the seasons with great majesty. So as an animal totem, the stag symbolizes strength, power and a deep connection to the Earth and her wisdom. This stone indicates incredible inner strength and encourages you to continue along your journey. You are being given the energy of survival at this time to help you adapt to the changes occurring and the environment around you. Stay true to yourself, your intuition and the guidance that is coming to you at this time.

Creating Your Own Warrior Stone Oracle

You are invited to create your very own warrior stone oracle so that you can connect to the guidance that is coming from your intuition and from the warrior guides who surround you. When you create an oracle, you place your own energy in it, so it becomes a direct reflection of your guidance system.

 Making Your Oracle

You can use almost anything to make your oracle – it needn't be stone. You can use nine little pieces of paper or card if you like, or even the little glass beads that people have in their plant pots. Whatever you have to hand is cool. I like the idea of using crystals because not only are they beautiful, but the energy of the symbols also becomes part of their energetic identity, but use what feels right to you.

All you need to create your oracle is a paint or pen that you know will go on any surface and nine stones or similar with a flat side (so that you can easily draw on the symbols), as well as a little pouch to keep them in.

You can make this oracle for next to nothing, but what it can offer you is priceless guidance from the wisdom that lies within.

Cleansing and Blessing Your Stones

If your stones have been lying around the house or you've just picked them up from a store, it would be a good idea to cleanse them so that there's no energy from elsewhere kicking around them (as this can throw off their accuracy) and they can become a vessel of your energy and intentions.

Cleansing

There are a couple of ways of doing this:

- Hold the stones under a running tap or a running stream and imagine that all the old energy within them is leaving and going down the drain or stream. You can then say:

  Spirit of water, thank you for clearing away all the old energy within these stones so that they become clear channels of light!

- Hold the stones over the smoke of burning incense, sage or palo santo and visualize it clearing all of the old energy out and imbuing the stones with the most sacred holy light. Say:

  Spirit of smoke, thank you for clearing all the old energy within these stones so that they become clear channels of light!

Blessing

- Holding the pouch containing your stones close to your heart, switch on your deep breathing and allow your heart energy to reach into the stones.

- Imagine that you are creating an immeasurable bond with the stones and that they have the capacity to mirror the sacred warrior voice within you.

- Then say:

  Mother Earth and Father Sky,

  Thank you for your blessings upon me and these stones. Thank you for allowing them to be a divine reflection of my intuition and of guidance coming from you.

By the powers of sun and moon, thank you for kissing these stones with your holiest light so that they will become a powerful bridge that brings the two worlds together.

Thank you for your blessings!

Aho!

You can also charge your stones in the light of the sun – be careful not to leave them too long, as this can make the paint fade on them – and the light of the moon.

How to Do a Reading

There are several ways to do a reading with your warrior stone oracle and I will explain them to you here.

Pouch Reading

This is the easiest way to ask for guidance.

- Holding the pouch that holds your warrior stones, take a moment to centre yourself and breathe deeply.

- If you have a question, don't make it a yes/no one, but ask for guidance on a particular situation.

- If you don't have a question, simply say, 'Thank you, warrior guidance, for revealing to me what I need to know.'

One-Stone Reading

This is the best way to receive overall guidance.

- Take a stone from the pouch.

- Spend time absorbing its message to you.

Three-Stone Reading

This will give you a deeper understanding of a situation.

- The first stone represents your strengths in the situation.

- The second stone represents your emotions in the situation.

- The third stone represents what you need to work on (challenge) in order for the situation to be resolved or healed.

⫸⟶ Casting Reading ⟵⫷

The casting of stones is a shamanic/seer practice found in all four corners of the world. It's super insightful and encourages you to use your intuition when combining the messages of the stones that are revealed during a reading.

I cast my stones on a small sheepskin, but you can also use a scarf folded up, or even soil in the garden or sand on the beach.

- Approach the stones in the same way as before, centring yourself with your breath and being open to what comes through.

- Holding all of the stones in your hand as you would a pair of dice, begin to shake them.

- Breathe life into them by exhaling directly onto them.

- Then say, 'Thank you, warrior guidance, for revealing to me what I need to know,' and throw them down to reveal your message.

- The stones that are facing upwards are your message. The stones closest to you show what needs your current attention and the stones furthest from you show action you need to take or guidance you need to follow.

Once the stones are cast, I recommend removing any that are face down, as they are not relevant in the reading.

If the stones all end up face down, your warrior guidance is to gather your thoughts and intentions and come back at a later time when you feel clearer.

When two stones overlap each other, facing upwards, this indicates a combined interpretation.

––––––––––

I have just cast my stones on the sheepskin that is at the bottom of my bed. I asked for general guidance on what I needed to know. Four stones are facing upwards.

The closest stone to me is the Arrow, so I know I have to remove any negative thinking from my energy in order to move along my light warrior path.

In the middle of the reading I have the Drum overlapping the Eagle. This combines the Drum's message of journeying and spiritual practice with the Eagle's message of gaining a higher perspective on the current situation. I can't help but feel that the warrior guidance is encouraging me to continue my journey with spirit and keep my focus on the higher perspective of this work.

The stone furthest from me is the Snake. The Snake brings the energy of change and renewal, because it sheds its old skin in order to reveal the vibrancy of what lies beneath. It can come to us when we have faced a fear, because it shows us the inner value of tackling what scares us the most. As the stone that's furthest away from me, it shows that there's an opportunity coming to reveal a deeper aspect of myself to the world.

This feels so powerful and accurate at this time. What's even more interesting is that last night I had a nightmare. Even though I thought I'd done my Psychic Protection 101, I'd been up late writing and then read a book on shamanic journeying before going to sleep, and it seems that I'd left myself too open (even us pro warriors forget). It feels as though this was a reminder from the spirit of my warrior self and my warrior guides to stay true to this path and do the journeying when I am safe and protected from any lower energy or any residual energy from the day. So cool!

Reading for Others

You can do warrior stone readings for others the same way as for yourself, except that when you're doing a reading for another person, let them say the prayer and pick/cast the stones.

Remember, the stones closest to them show what they need to work on now and those furthest from them indicate either what requires action on their part or guidance coming through.

I find that sitting beside someone and looking at the stones with them is more helpful than sitting across the table or room from them.

When you have finished the reading, thank the heavens and thank the Earth for all that was received. Gratitude keeps the channels open and clear.

Warrior Workout

~ Set time aside to work with your intuition in meditation.

~ Spend some time working out whether any old intentions could be standing between you and greatness. If so, you know what to do!

~ Work with your favourite oracle cards or invest in a set to which you feel drawn.

~ Create your own warrior stone oracle and practise doing readings for yourself or your loved ones.

Chapter 10
STEPPING INTO SERVICE

'The fruit of service is peace.'
MOTHER TERESA

In my opinion, and I'm sure you'll agree, one of the greatest light warriors of our time is His Holiness the Dalai Lama. What an incredible man – he is so well loved and respected around the world, and my goodness, he has worked so hard to make a difference.

I had the pleasure of hearing him speak in Edinburgh a few years ago and I was amazed by the gigantic angels of light who were all around him. These were beings of pure love and compassion and I knew that they were helping him to do his sacred work.

In case you're not fully aware of what the Dalai Lama does, I want to take a moment just to share with you some of his greatness, because I feel his work encourages the light to emerge in so many people, and if we can do even a fraction of the light work that he has done, then we will be doing big things in the world.

Tenzin Gyatso, the 14th Dalai Lama, is one of the most influential leaders of peace in the world today. Not only is he the main dude in Tibetan Buddhism, he is also the leader of Tibet, although, just like many other Tibetans, he fled to India in 1959 because of threats to his life from the communist government of China.

Although right now there is struggle and great suffering in Tibet, and I know the Dalai Lama feels that, he dedicates himself to travelling around the world, inspiring everyone from schoolchildren to religious leaders and even world leaders with his advocacy of human rights and compassion.

Every day he wakes at 4 or 5 a.m. to devote himself to his spiritual practice. When he won the Nobel Peace Prize in 1989, in his acceptance speech he described himself as a simple monk and declared that his sacred work had been nurtured by his focus on prayer, meditation and gratitude.

We have to be inspired by great light warriors like the Dalai Lama and the service he has given to the world.

Serving Ourselves, Serving Others

Like the Dalai Lama, we must dedicate time to ourselves and our spiritual practice and then we, too, can bring light to the world. Through our own awareness, we can help create awareness in the world. Through our own healing, we can share healing with others. Through focusing on peace in our own life, we can bring peace into the world.

The great Hindu text the *Bhagavad Gita* says, 'True sustenance comes from service,' and I'm sure you'll agree it feels incredible to help others. Being a light warrior is all about helping others, but helping them in the best way – from a place of fullness and energy rather than tiredness and depletion.

I know that there are many people struggling to continue serving others because they are *completely* – mentally, emotionally and spiritually – exhausted. I was one of those people and I want to share that. It has taken me a long time to get to where I am now in my life – filled with purpose and finding a balance between self-service and service to others.

I've come to see that many of us in the spiritual world feel the need to be of service, and because we feel that need, we try to respond to it. We ask the universe in our prayers and our practice how we can be of service, yet we find ourselves in jobs we don't like or places where we aren't energized – why? It's simple, and you know the answer already: we're getting what we're asking for.

Like many on this path, I've often moved into prayer to ask how I can be of service. Daily for years I would say, 'Universe, show me how I can be of service,' and, 'Thank you, universe, for using my life to serve you.'

I said these prayers daily when I started my business and they helped me establish what I do today, there's no doubt of that, but somewhere along the way I reached burnout, because I was essentially being used to my maximum capacity. I was seeing sometimes 40 clients in one week, and to be honest, although many people were being helped, it wasn't helping me. I had to figure out why.

The realization of what was happening came to me not when I was working with myself, but when I was working with a client.

Polly had been interested in spiritual work for over a decade, but was still working in the corporate world. She had done many different types of spiritual training, from energy work to oracle card reading certification, and had attended many of my angel clubs. She longed to do spiritual work and when she finally hit a brick wall in her work life, she came to me for guidance on how she could be of service.

I remember taking a moment to check in with the angels and saying, 'Dear angels, thank you for revealing what Polly needs to do in order to feel more of service and fulfilled.'

Instantly a voice came into my mind – it was my own inner voice but I know it was angelically inspired – and it said, 'The universe is giving Polly what she asked for. She never asked to be fulfilled, she just asked to be of service.'

And thud, that was it. Not only was Polly's message so true and so powerful, it was also the message I needed to hear.

The 'use me, let me be of service' prayer is essentially the road to burnout. The universe isn't complicated – it gives us everything we ask for if we keep our intentions strong and focused or if we repeatedly ask for the same thing. If we ask it to use us, then it absolutely will.

That's why many lightworkers are facing burnout – because they're being sent to where they are needed. Most great lights in this world are sent to the darkest places, because that's where their light can be of maximum service. But is it serving them?

As lightworkers and light warriors, we need to recognize that *we* have to be served as we step into service. If we ask to live a life of service then we will live a life of service, but we may not feel fulfilled by it. If we want to feel fulfilled by it, we have to ask for that too.

I remember feeding all this back to Polly and it made complete sense to her. She was being of service to the staff at her corporate job – daily she would have people arriving at her desk to ask for advice, share a secret, speak about a challenge or just offload emotionally – but she felt they were taking her kindness and compassion for granted. It definitely wasn't serving her.

I told her that I, too, had had similar experiences and we both agreed it was definitely time to change our intentions.

I guided Polly to declare to the universe that she was ready to change her intentions and clear away the old ones.

If we want to change the plan, we do need to tell the universe about it, because if we don't, it starts getting mixed messages and therefore provides muddled experiences.

I've since upgraded the declaration I took Polly through that day and I'm going to share with you my most up-to-date service prayer. May this prayer lead you to a more purpose-filled, joyful experience of service.

✗ *Prayer for Joyful Service*

Dear universe and warrior guides,

I come here in humility and honesty to make a declaration.

I am ready to release my old intentions to be of service because I am ready to create new ones.

Thank you for clearing, cancelling and deleting all the old intentions of service I have previously made.

Thank you for all the opportunities to serve I have had up to this point, but know that I am now ready to upgrade my energy and my offering. I am ready to experience fulfilment and purpose *through service.*

Thank you, universe, for showing me how I can serve the world in a way that serves me.

Thank you, warrior guides, for leading me safely along this path to opportunities that will allow me to light up as never before.

I am ready to be a beacon of light. I am ready to experience utter joy as I shine. I welcome all levels of abundance, I welcome all levels of guidance and I welcome all levels of purpose.

Thank you, greatness within me, for standing at the forefront of my mind and my heart and leading me towards this joy.

Thank you, thank you, thank you.

And so it is.

Make this prayer part of your daily practice and let your service be full of joy.

This is why the previous chapters in this book have been about mental, emotional and psychic preparation – so that you have the tools in place to do the work you want to do *in a way that fulfils you.*

I've also pushed heavily that it's okay to say 'no', and I think it's important to share this message here again, because I feel that so many lightworkers have felt obliged to serve rather than been inspired to do so.

You always have a choice. Spirit wants to help you help

others, but it won't rely on you to be the only answer to a situation. So don't feel it's always down to you.

If you do feel that you can give in a way that lights you up, however, follow that call. You'll align with the spirit of purpose, and that feeling of purpose will raise your frequency so high!

Let's Talk Life Purpose

Talking of purpose, like many other lightworkers and warriors, I've spent a long time searching for answers to some of the bigger questions in life. One of the quests I've been on is to gain a deeper understanding of what life purpose really means. What are we here for? Is it to serve in some way? How can we find out?

When I wrote my first book, I wrote a whole chapter on life purpose. I was 21 then, and even though I had a lot of knowledge about angels, there were still some things that I wasn't fully clear on. Life purpose was one of them. Back then I was convinced that our life purpose was also our career, or connected directly to it, and boy, was I wrong! Life purpose is much simpler than that.

> **According to *A Course in Miracles*, our function – our
> life purpose – is salvation, forgiveness and happiness.**

What does this mean? I've come to believe that through a daily spiritual practice (salvation), which naturally includes forgiveness, we can fulfil our life purpose, which is to be happy.

This means that our career can never be our true purpose, although it can contribute to it. Knowing this takes any unnecessary pressure off us. The universe doesn't have a job role for us, it simply wants us to experience happiness and share happiness.

So, relax. You don't need your dream job in order to fulfil your life purpose. It helps, obviously – doing this sacred work, speaking about spirituality and writing books like this gives me a great sense of joy and therefore I feel my work is 'on purpose' – but you can be happy in so many ways, not only through your career.

**Your life purpose is to be happy and
you are encouraged to share that
happiness everywhere you go.**

Have you been putting too much energy or effort into what you thought was your 'divine life purpose' and forgetting to be happy along the way? It's time to lift the weight of responsibility from your shoulders, because it's standing between you and your real life purpose – *to be happy*.

✕ *Happiness Prayer*

*Thank you, universe and angels, for removing the pressure
I have allowed to stand between me and happiness. Today I
choose to take the weight of the world from my shoulders so
that I can unite with my greatness.*

And so it is.

Our Natural State of Being

We can choose to be happy, but happiness isn't something we can force or create within ourselves. But there's a very special reason for that – it's already there, waiting for us to uncover it. It's our natural state of being.

I was recently working alongside the well-respected psychic medium Gordon Smith. This guy is the real deal and has helped thousands of grieving people by bringing through messages from their loved ones in spirit. During one of our conversations, he mentioned that spirit was *a state of being* that was inside us, and when our body died, we would return to that state. He said that it was a state of complete bliss, contentment, connectedness and love.

That state is essentially what we're all looking for. Jesus called it 'ascension', Buddha called it 'enlightenment' and it's known as *samadhi* or *nirvana* in Hinduism.

A Course in Miracles points out that to teach is to learn, which I take to mean that as we begin to work with this energy and help others reach this state of happiness and love, we'll also uncover it inside ourselves.

Warrior Workout

~ Take some time to set up some daily intentions to serve your own happiness.

~ Meditate on the idea that your happiness is serving the healing of the world.

~ Take any extra pressure off your shoulders regarding your life purpose.

~ Create a vision of what would be supportive of your own happiness.

~ Upgrade your daily service prayer with the one suggested here or create one in your own authentic voice.

Chapter 11
EMBODY THE WARRIOR

'A warrior seeks to act rather than talk.'
CARLOS CASTANEDA

The real warrior is within. You don't become a warrior – you already are one. At this point my prayer is that you are beginning to emerge from the cave of fear into the light of your soul. My prayer is that you will begin to be the warrior you were born to be.

Being a light warrior is a calling. It's almost like being recruited, only not to learn a new skill or to undergo training, just to become who you really are. I believe that the greatest light work anyone can do in this world is fully be themselves, because then they are contributing integrity and authenticity to the oneness of life of which we are all a part.

All of the tools and ideas shared in this book will support you in consciously embodying your light warrior. The daily practice of facing fear, connecting to your guidance system and remembering the love you are will help you to step into your warrior self and reveal that to the world.

**Becoming fully embodied is about fearlessly
walking your talk, knowing that you are
never separate from the divine.**

I believe I began to reveal my warrior self during my first trip to India.

I went to India on a wild pilgrimage. I'd just finished writing my book Angels and this month-long retreat was everything I'd dreamed about. I'd wanted to go to India ever since I'd learned about Hinduism at school. I wanted to see the temples, walk the incense-filled streets and become one with the hustle and bustle. I was ready to bow down, I was ready to prostrate myself, I was ready to learn.

I booked myself into an ashram that had a modern-day spiritual teacher, thinking he would take me closer to self-mastery. I'd totally bought into the idea that this wildly spiritual country and this guru dressed in white, with a big beard and long hair, would bring me something 'special'.

In a way, they did.

The weirdest thing happened the day I arrived – I broke out from head to toe in hives. Huge hives. They stayed for a whole week. I didn't realize at the time that it was a full-body response. My body either didn't want me to be there or it was giving me the opportunity to take this journey (and all it entailed) or not. When I look back, I understand why.

There were a lot of things happening in that ashram that didn't sit well with me. We were told that it was sacred ground and we had to respect it, but let's just say that rule wasn't being adhered to by the 'guru' who was in charge.

The first thing that really horrified me was when one of the staff brought a stray puppy to the ashram (you know there are so many in India) and the teacher asked them to 'remove it'. They took him all the way out onto the main road and let him go. A puppy left by the side of the road? Not in my name.

I didn't hold back. 'You have one hour to find that puppy and bring him back here or I will get very cross!'

Ooops. One hour passed. Then a whole night. For me, it was a restless night. I lay in my small room, on my very hard bed, wondering what I was going to do about it. The warrior within wasn't going to sit around and do nothing. But what?

The next day, the puppy was back. Thank God, because I really have no idea what I would have done otherwise.

But I continued to feel uncomfortable. There was a 'jaggy vibe', as my mother calls it, in the air. I just wasn't enjoying my time there. I stopped going to the communal meetings and yoga and confined myself to my room and my own spiritual practice.

I also became pretty sure that there was a lot more going on than there should be.

After a while I just wasn't prepared to continue letting things slip by. I went to the teacher and asked if I could speak with him privately. I wanted to respect him and

I wanted to receive his respect in return. I called in my angels, asked them to hold me close and began to share my truth.

I told the teacher that I had reason to believe he was having sexual relations with students and that I didn't feel it was professional. I also told him that I didn't like what had happened with the dog and that it didn't feel as though he was acting with integrity.

I was surprised by what he said in return.

'You are in a deep state of maya [illusion]. Because of the powerful energy of the ashram and the cleanses in the yogas, you are now going through a state of maya and this is what has created these ideas.'

'Are you kidding me?' I said.

He looked puzzled. His cover-up technique wasn't working.

'I'm not falling for this,' I went on. 'In a supposedly "sacred place" like this you can actually look me in the eye and think I'm going to believe this lie? I believe we all have illusions to face, but for goodness' sake, it's obvious what's happening here and I will never be a part of it. I'll be leaving in the morning.'

There was a lot more I could have said, but I ended the conversation there, because I knew I was never going to get the closure I was seeking.

As I walked to the communal kitchen area, I saw the little puppy playing around. He made me smile. At that moment of disillusionment, he brought me joy and hope.

One of the staff members who was a Krishna devotee was in the kitchen. Suddenly he picked up a massive cane and hit the dog – in front of the whole group.

I couldn't believe it. I kicked off my flip flops and before I knew it I'd taken the guy down to the floor, my foot was on his throat and I was staring ferociously into his eyes.

'If you hit that dog again, I'll hit you!' I screamed. 'I can't believe you're all going on about being vegetarian to stop animal suffering and you're treating this baby dog like a piece of shit! I will not witness this fucking behaviour!'

I'd never in my life been so enraged yet so empowered. My true warrior self had truly been brought to the surface.

It reminded me of the goddess Kali-Ma (more about her later) standing on the god Shiva and commanding his respect. She took on the most powerful god there was as an initiation into her own power. The image of Kali standing on Shiva is emblematic of the more sensitive, receptive side rising up and out – it's a symbol of fearless power. I was full of fearless power right then.

The man couldn't even speak a word of English and I knew that he'd been exposed to so much of that sort of behaviour that it was normal for him. I just hope I gave him a wake-up call. And the entire group as well. No one supported me or even said anything to me – they just stared in what I can only describe as amazement.

I took my foot off the man's throat and retreated to my room. And I sobbed, deeply. I was tired and frustrated and

I felt betrayed. But at the same time I had a glimmer of realization: this was an initiation into my own power.

Later that night, as I snacked on the health bars and corn chips I had stashed in my bag, one by one people came to my door – other students wanting to 'see if I was okay' but really coming to thank me. They told me they'd been too scared to say anything about the things that had been taking place and two women revealed they had been inappropriately touched.

The next morning I prepared to leave and so did many others. My light warrior initiation had given them the confidence to take their own power back. Three taxis full of pilgrims left that day. The five-hour drive through towns, villages and farmland felt like the most incredible journey to freedom ever!

For those of you wondering about the dog, I paid one of the workers at the ashram to look after him and they sent me regular photos for a year. Eventually I decided to cut all ties, but I've seen things about him occasionally on social media. Essentially, I've had to trust that he has his journey and I have mine. But I know he is well.

That powerful experience taught me something I already knew but still hadn't fully realized: all that I was looking for was already within me. Somewhere during the course of reading books on India and yoga I'd got caught up in the idea that by going to India I was going to get 'something special' or be made 'more special' than I already was. *That* idea was the *maya* I was facing.

**Gone are the days when we need a guru.
We are here to be our own guide.**

That journey helped me uncover the warrior within, but that was something that was always there.

There is a warrior within us all. When we choose to live a life of integrity, open to guidance, filled with spiritual kinship and love for ourselves and others, we embody that warrior.

I know by the fact that you are here right now, on this page, reading this book and doing this work, that you are already a light warrior.

The warrior in me bows to the warrior in you.

I'm proud of you. You should be proud of yourself too.

Embodiments of Fierceness

I've always been interested in deities, especially the deities of Hinduism and Buddhism. What I've always loved about them is that they are all extensions of the divine. All the different gods of India are ultimately one with the main force of creation and it's the same with the deities in Buddhism.

For many years I've loved calling upon deities just as I've called on angels. I've often viewed them as 'up there' to be honest, but in more recent times I've recognized that they're all parts of the divinity *within*. So I ask them to help me with awakening certain aspects of myself, generally based on the aspects they themselves display in the spiritual tales and sagas.

Never look outside yourself – dive deep within!

I want to introduce you to two of my favourite 'wrathful deities'. A wrathful deity is an enlightened intelligence that takes on a fierce form in order to lead sentient beings towards mastery. In the Mahayana and Vajrayana schools of Buddhism, these deities are often manifestations of *bodhisattvas*. They are the protectors of sacred teachings and the defenders of the light. They are often depicted as scary creatures adorned with bones and skulls. (Don't we all have a side of us that can be quite scary at times?) Ultimately, though, they are just personifications of the fierce protective love that is within us.

Mahakala

Mahakala is one of the wrathful deities in Tibetan Buddhism. His name means 'beyond time and death'. He has four arms, three eyes, and is of the brilliance of 10 million black fires. He is adorned with skulls and seated on corpses. He holds various weapons, including a trident and a scythe. He is one of the protectors of the Buddha and the sacred teachings of Buddhism.

Mahakala helps us look directly into the eyes of fear so we can move beyond all of the attachments, dramas and limitations that stop us from expressing our own brilliance. He is a destroyer of illusion. He is about unleashing the untamed self so that we can be ourselves authentically and completely.

Kali-Ma

Kali-Ma is a Hindu goddess and one of the fiercest deities ever. This blue-skinned lady with eight arms filled with weapons, wearing a tiger skin, a skull necklace and standing on top of

Shiva is not to be messed with. Her name also means 'beyond time and death' and she is the great mother, destroyer of 'evil' and fear.

Kali-Ma can make us feel safe, like a protective mother, but she can also awaken the fierce protector within. She can guide us to eliminate self-destructive patterns, tame angry thoughts and take a stand in negative situations.

Mahakala-Kali-Ma, Conjoined as One

Although these two deities feature in different religions, they are said to be divine counterparts. They symbolize the divine masculine and the divine feminine. One cannot exist without the other. They need each other to grow.

As well as representing the divine power to destroy illusion and move beyond fear, they help us recognize that we all, men and women, have that power within us and can embody it. Conjoined, they allow us to conjure up the power to stand in our own light and ultimately be a light to the world.

⟫⟶ Mahakala-Kali *Kriya* ⟵⟪ with Roaring Breath

Kriya is the Sanskrit for 'physical manifestation'. In the Mahakala-Kali *Kriya* (sounds the way it looks: ma, ha, ka, la, ka, li, kree yaaa), you will bring together breath, movement, posture, sound and visualization to help you dial up an internal warrior connection that will free you from venom and allow you to step into your fiercest, most protective power.

Using the roaring breath, you will combine a yoga pose flow with hand movements to boost your energy system and unlock the warrior within.

You can add this *kriya* to your yoga practice or bring it into ceremony. I've also used it when I've been in a space that doesn't feel friendly – where there is old energy lurking in hotels, for example. It's great – I just charge myself up and take my power back!

Please read through the whole *kriya* before you start.

1. Start by taking star pose:

    ~ Stand with your feet about four feet (just over a metre) apart and turn your heels in about 45 degrees.

    ~ Remain soft through your knees to protect your joints.

    ~ Spread your arms out to the side, with your palms facing down and your shoulders strong.

Star pose

2. Inhale using the Ujjayi breath (*see page 21*).

3. As you exhale, sink deep into Goddess pose, phase 1:

   ~ Exhale as you bend your knees and move into a wide-leg squat. Aim to keep your tailbone tucked under and feet active (push down on all four corners of your feet for stability).

   ~ Bring your hands to your thighs with your fingers pointing backwards and your elbow crease soft and facing forward, shoulders rolling back and shoulder blades down.

4. As you do so, exhale using the hissing sound from the roaring breath (*see page 40*; save the roars for phase 2).

Goddess pose with hands to thighs, phase 1

5. Then inhale (continuing your Ujjayi breathing) and move your arms up into *Apaan mudra*:

~ Turn your hands up while retaining a slight bend in the elbow.

~ Press your second and third fingers against your thumb while raising your first and little fingers (which is actually the 'rock on' sign you see people doing at rock shows).

Apaan mudra

Apa or *Apaan* is said to mean 'outward' or 'exhalation'. *Apaan mudra* is said to bring your power out from the inside.

6. As you do this, begin to straighten your legs.

7. Hold your breath. Imagine all of your venom preparing to leave your body.

8. Bend your knees into Goddess pose, phase 2:

9. In one large exhale, stick out your tongue and *roar* out with a loud 'Ha!' all of your venom to reveal the light warrior within.

Goddess pose with *Apaan mudra*, phase 2

10. Repeat three to five times.

Tantric Embodiment

Now don't get your knickers in a twist here – I'm not talking about tantric sex, I'm talking about tantric meditation. Tantric meditation is simply meditating to awaken kundalini energy, which is essentially the energy of cosmic creation, in yourself. When you draw that energy up your body from its resting place at the foot of your spine, you unite with the divine.

In many schools of thought, including Vajrayana Buddhism, there is the idea that you can visualize yourself as a certain deity, master, Buddha and guide in order to awaken their qualities within you. So in tantric meditation you can use the energy of creation to visualize yourself as Mahakala–Kali-Ma and awaken the fierce warrior within.

➤━━━━➤ Tantric Embodiment Meditation ◄━━━◄

You can do this meditation as often as you like. The fierceness it creates is actually anything but angry - it's a fierce love that will overcome fear.

I recommend familiarizing yourself with the steps before taking yourself through it. You might like to record it so that you can move through it easily.

- After performing Mahakala-Kali *Kriya* (*see above*), assume a comfortable seated position.

- Begin your deepest Ujjayi warrior breathing. Remain with this breath throughout.

- Imagine a light in the centre of your being. It may seem dim, so encourage it to glow brightly. See it growing larger and brighter until it covers the entirety of your being.

- This light begins to attract an incredible deity of fierce light.

- See in your mind the manifestation of Mahakala-Kali-Ma (male, female or both) before you.

- Invite this presence to step into your being. See this as a welcoming back of something that has always been there, but has just lain dormant for a while.

- See powerful energy buzzing around your body.

- Feel the fierce love within you pulsating through the whole of your being.

- Imagine your soul rising up within, strong, full and fearless.

- When you feel this process is complete, open your eyes and say:

    I am awakened, embodied and aligned. I am a warrior filled with the fiercest light and love!

You may want to do some more Mahakala–Kali *Kriyas* to cement this sacred work. Then dance to your favourite music.

Warrior Workout

~ Look back over your life and pick out any moments when you stood strong and fierce. Was that your warrior self awakening?

~ Think back to times when you looked for an answer outside yourself, then finally found it within.

~ Check out online images of Mahakala and Kali-Ma to familiarize yourself with their energy.

~ Practise the tantric embodiment meditation to fill yourself with fierce love.

Chapter 12
DO THE WORK

*'You are what you do, not
what you say you'll do.'*
CARL JUNG

Right now I see the spiritual community going through a massive shift. More people are awakening than ever before and it's become cool to be spiritual. This is something that I'm grateful for, but many of them don't know where to start. So light warrior work is needed more than ever.

You have consciously chosen to be here at this time, to raise your vibration and to answer the call for light. You have chosen to actively bring change to the world and spread light wherever you can. So this is a call to action.

You know now that the way to respond to the call for light is to deal with your own darkness and transform your own fear. It would be really easy if you could just switch into love, light and unicorn mode, but ultimately no amount of positive thinking will ever undo the negative. Authentically aligning yourself with the light can only be done through facing the darkness.

The techniques in this book will provide you with a solid foundation on which you can base your spiritual practice. They will guide you through to the light.

So step onto this path and do the work. Your angels and guides will support you, but you must make that commitment. Recognize right now that no certification, no initiation, no teacher, no guru, no temple and no secrets will ever do it for you, or make you more spiritual than you already are – you are spirit and that's it. As are we all.

Gone are the days when we can cover up fear of the world by learning another healing art. We have to dive deep within, uncover the stuff we're carrying around and bring it into the light.

And we have to recognize that this service to ourselves is ultimately service to the whole. It is the work of a light warrior.

Dealing with Persecution

It's only fair to say that this work isn't always easy. One big thing that comes up when many light warriors finally start to do the work is an energy of confrontation and resistance – I call it *persecution*.

So many of my spiritual friends and colleagues have found themselves in the firing line when they have begun to make a difference with their work and I've also experienced a great deal of resistance in the past from people who didn't agree with my beliefs or my message.

For thousands of years spiritual leaders have been persecuted because of their presence and their power, because many people feel threatened by the prospect of change.

The greatest light warrior who was persecuted for his work was Jesus. As you know, I love Jesus – he's the fiercest form of love I know. He was nailed to a cross because others simply didn't agree with his message and his beliefs.

All over the world people doing great spiritual work have been branded as bad, evil, witches or charlatans. As late as World War II, an incredible Scottish medium named Helen Duncan was falsely accused of being a witch and a spy because of her sheer accuracy, and was imprisoned under the Witchcraft Act. Today, even the Dalai Lama has to face the Chinese government and certain Buddhist sects claiming he is a false prophet and a demon, although the work he does speaks for itself.

This persecution – this old fear and old energy – has to end once and for all. Enough have died, enough have suffered and enough have been slandered, and now we must declare that we are letting this old energy go so that we can step into the light.

I believe that herbalists, healers, mediums, white witches and prophets of the past are reincarnating in these times because this is when it is possible to make a difference. I believe when we're afraid of coming out of the spiritual closet – of emerging as lightworkers and light warriors – we're feeling the fear of souls long past.

An inner shift has to occur – a new way of thinking, a new way of allowing.

It's time to bring the miracle that's required.

If you meet with resistance or feel as though you're being persecuted for your beliefs, or even if you're just afraid that you will be, know that there's been enough suffering already and the change *must* come from you.

When you feel that energy of resistance, fear or persecution, you have the opportunity to transform it. Every time you feel someone or something is trying to get in the way of your growth, including your own fear, this is the prayer for you. Use it as many times as you need it.

✕ *Prayer for Freedom from Persecution*

Universe, this is a declaration.

I am not here to be persecuted in this lifetime.

There has been enough suffering and fear already in the lives of my ancestors and the great teachers who have gone before me.

Today I vow to release all fears or experiences of persecution. The darkness of fear will not stand in the way of my light.

I declare that I am unbound.

I am seen and acknowledged for my light and for my capacity to bring healing changes to the world.

I let my light lead the way.

I am light. I am love. I am free.

Holding the Light

Around the time I began putting my ideas together to write this book, I was speaking at the Angel World Summit 2016 in London. I was excited at the prospect of sharing my ideas with so many people, but then the morning before the summit, the Brexit result was announced, and bam, how unexpected was that? It felt strange. I'm not using this space to share political ideas, but the prospect of Britain leaving the EU meant that there was huge uncertainty in the air.

I knew that I was going to be speaking about what it meant to be a light warrior, but I'd no idea how I was going to make it make sense at such a moment.

I decided to do what I always do when I don't know the answer to something. No, not google. Meditate.

I dropped down into meditation right there. Sitting on the floor of my hotel room, I flipped my hands up, took Pran mudra and closed my eyes. I just said internally, 'Angels, I need a miracle!' Remember, a miracle is a shift in perception.

I breathed deeply for a few minutes, bathing myself from head to toe in light, and then it came, like a gust of wind – an air of inspiration blew over me.

I recognized that I wasn't alone. I could feel angels circling me and I knew they knew I was dedicating this miracle to service.

And then the answer came: 'In times of uncertainty, you must hold the light!'

There it was, the medicine I needed. Why hadn't I thought of that? Because fear is what we are programmed with in this world, including fear of the unknown.

But now I'd experienced a miracle and was already turning my thoughts, my energy and my life back to the light.

Whenever you face uncertainty, hold the light.

Whenever you're filled with fear, whenever you're unsure of what to do next, meditate, receive and move back into the light. Take refuge in the light. The light is who you truly are. Come back to that and you'll be given the answers you need.

A Final Word on Service

Now, before you go out and do the work, I feel this is so important: I'm giving you just one more reminder about what it means to serve.

Serving Yourself

Doing the work means serving yourself.

I'm not saying live a self-centred life, but I'm encouraging you to serve yourself before you serve others. For hundreds of years the lightworker path has been about self-sacrifice and this needs to change. In order for our work to truly be successful, we cannot be wounded or unhealed healers.

> *'When I am healed, I am not healed alone.'*
> A Course in Miracles

Through serving yourself, healing yourself and facing your own fears, you will teach others to do the same. Through respecting and loving yourself, you will give permission and encouragement to all those who need to do the same.

Through having the integrity to say 'no' when you mean 'no', you will help others become empowered.

**Whatever you do for yourself is what
you offer up to the world.**

So, face your fears. Call on your angels and guides for the support you need. Delve deep into ceremony and delve deep into your soul. Recognize the warrior within.

Connect with your intuition and be clear about where you want it to lead you. Make your intentions known. Whenever you feel that your prayers haven't been heard, pray for clarity. Whenever things don't go the way you thought they would, trust that you are being led to a deeper sense of connection.

Declare that you are free and are not here to be persecuted. This is not a quick ride – this is a life-long journey and you must enjoy it.

Serving Others

When you serve yourself, you are ultimately serving others anyway, and from a place that is true and authentic. But you can serve others directly if you feel called to do so.

- Serve others through your love. Show how deeply you love those in your life.

- Serve others through forgiveness. If someone has made a mistake, don't make them pay – heal yourself and move on.

- Serve others through honesty. If something needs to be said, pray for insight and support, then share your truth.

- Serve others through sharing. Share everything you learn and everything you can do. Show others how. This is how you will heal the world.

- Serve others through thanks. Give thanks to your teachers, the good and the bad. Thank them for their lessons and then share your own teachings.

When you serve others, know that whatever you give out will come back to you. If payment or energetic exchange doesn't come directly from those you have helped, it will come in another form.

Serving the Earth

I believe that just by being on Earth we have a purpose: to respect this incredible planet. We are not the owners of the Earth, but guests, and we have to respect our host.

Indigenous peoples in the four corners of the world have long recognized the Earth as the Great Mother. Today modern-day pagans, shamans and eco-friendly spiritual practitioners are recognizing that the Earth needs us more than ever.

In his book *The Way of the Shaman*, Michael Harner speaks about the importance of creating a direct bond with the Earth:

> *Our ancient hunting and gathering ancestors recognized that their environment held the power of life and death over them, and considered such communication essential for their survival.*

Every day the Earth gives us a path to walk along. She gives us a home; she feeds us, nourishes us, gives us water to drink and air to breathe. For these reasons alone, I believe it's important to create a loving connection to her.

Just recently during an event, a lady asked me a question on the healing of the Earth and what we could do to help, and I received a message from my guides loud and clear: *'You are your ancestors' prayers being answered.'*

That message is a strong and powerful one for us all. For thousands of years our ancestors have been praying to the higher power for healing, for peace and for change. I believe every generation that has followed those prayers has been an opportunity for that healing to manifest. We now are our ancestors' answered prayers and we owe it to them and ourselves to make that change so that future generations can know a world that is filled with goodness. It is down to us.

Every day you can place your feet on the ground (even if it's inside your home) and imagine the soles of your feet kissing the Earth. Then say a prayer of thanks to her. Here is mine:

Prayer of Thanks to the Earth

Thank you, thank you, thank you, Mother Earth,

Thank you for holding me, for hosting me and for giving me a path to walk along,

Thank you for your plants, your animals and all your blessings.

I am so grateful to be part of you!

Here are some suggestions for creating a loving bond with Mother Nature:

- Love her animals.

- Love her plants.

- Love her people.

- Respect the land on which you walk. Clean it wherever possible.

- Use less plastic.

- Recycle where possible.

- Choose food that is organic.

- Give thanks to the plants you consume.

- If you eat meat or fish, choose animals who have lived as naturally as possible and thank them for surrendering their life for your nourishment.

- Do not ignore desecration and pollution of the Earth. If you don't know how to help, ask someone. We can all work together.

Live life from the light and the light will lead the way.

You are a light warrior and you were born to shine.

RECOMMENDED READING

Inner Work

Louise Hay, *You Can Heal Your Life*, Hay House, 1984
Doreen Virtue, *The Lightworker's Way*, Hay House, 1997

Earth Magic and Shamanism

Philip Carr-Gomm, *The Druid Animal Oracle*, Connections, 1996
Michael Drake, *The Shamanic Drum*, Talking Drum, 2002
Ana T. Forrest, *Fierce Medicine*, HarperCollins, 2011
Michael Harner, *The Way of the Shaman*, Harper & Row, 1980
Christa Mackinnon, *Shamanism*, Hay House, 2016
Alberto Villoldo, *Shaman, Healer*, Sage, Bantam, 2001
Kate West, *The Real Witches' Book of Spells and Rituals*, Element, 2003

Eastern Wisdom Meets the West

Mahātmā Gandhi and Richard Attenborough, *The Words of Gandhi*, Newmarket Press, 2000

Thích Nhất Hạnh, *Love Letter to the Earth*, Parallax Press, 2013

Chögyam Trungpa, Shambhala: *The Sacred Path of the Warrior*, Shambhala, 1984

—, *Smile at Fear: Awakening the True Heart of Bravery*, Shambhala, 2010

Paramahansa Yogananda, *Autobiography of a Yogi*, 1946, Self-Realization Fellowship, 1998

ABOUT THE AUTHOR

Drew John Barnes

Kyle Gray is an intuitive and angel expert who has been acknowledged for his remarkable spiritual connection, and has become one of the most sought-after experts in his field. With his unique ability to stay grounded and keep it real, he reintroduces angels and ancient spiritual knowledge in a modern way that allows these vast subjects to become approachable. He believes angels and the divine aren't just for a certain type of person but for everyone – angels are all inclusive.

Growing up, Kyle had an ability to hear, feel and see what goes beyond the natural senses, and experienced spiritual encounters from an early age. When he was just four years old, and following being paralysed with a virus, his grandmother's soul visited him from the other side. During his teens he discovered the power of magic and the love of angels.

Now, Kyle speaks all over the world, and his talks in the UK and Europe often sell out. He is based in Glasgow, Scotland, where he where he enjoys yoga and CrossFit, and dining out.

f **KyleGrayUK**

🐦 **@KyleGrayUK**

📷 **KyleGrayUK**

www.kylegray.co.uk

We hope you enjoyed this Hay House book. If you'd like
to receive our online catalog featuring additional information on
Hay House books and products, or if you'd like to find out more
about the Hay Foundation, please contact:

Hay House, Inc., P.O. Box 5100, Carlsbad, CA 92018-5100
(760) 431-7695 or (800) 654-5126
(760) 431-6948 (fax) or (800) 650-5115 (fax)
www.hayhouse.com® • www.hayfoundation.org

Published and distributed in Australia by: Hay House Australia Pty. Ltd.,
18/36 Ralph St., Alexandria NSW 2015 • *Phone:* 612-9669-4299
Fax: 612-9669-4144 • www.hayhouse.com.au

Published and distributed in the United Kingdom by:
Hay House UK, Ltd., Astley House, 33 Notting Hill Gate,
London W11 3JQ • *Phone:* 44-20-3675-2450
Fax: 44-20-3675-2451 • www.hayhouse.co.uk

Published and distributed in the Republic of South Africa by:
Hay House SA (Pty), Ltd., P.O. Box 990, Witkoppen 2068 •
info@hayhouse.co.za • www.hayhouse.co.za

Published in India by: Hay House Publishers India, Muskaan Complex,
Plot No. 3, B-2, Vasant Kunj, New Delhi 110 070 • *Phone:* 91-11-4176-1620
Fax: 91-11-4176-1630 • www.hayhouse.co.in

Distributed in Canada by: Raincoast Books,
2440 Viking Way, Richmond, B.C. V6V 1N2
Phone: 1-800-663-5714 • *Fax:* 1-800-565-3770 • www.raincoast.com

---

Access New Knowledge.
Anytime. Anywhere.

Learn and evolve at your own pace with the world's leading experts.

www.hayhouseU.com